THE QUOTABLE SPIRIT

THE
QUOTABLE
SPIRIT

Quotations of Wisdom and Grace

Compiled and Edited by Peter Lorie
and Manuela Dunn Mascetti

STERLING INNOVATION
An imprint of Sterling Publishing Co., Inc.

New York / London
www.sterlingpublishing.com

STERLING, the Sterling logo, STERLING INNOVATION,
and the Sterling Innovation logo are registered trademarks
of Sterling Publishing Co., Inc.

Library of Congress Cataloging-in-Publication Data Available

10 9 8 7 6 5 4 3 2 1

Published by Sterling Publishing Co., Inc.
387 Park Avenue South, New York, NY 10016

© 2010 by Sterling Publishing Co., Inc.

Distributed in Canada by Sterling Publishing
c/o Canadian Manda Group, 165 Dufferin Street
Toronto, Ontario, Canada M6K 3H6
Distributed in the United Kingdom by GMC Distribution Services
Castle Place, 166 High Street, Lewes, East Sussex, England BN7 1XU
Distributed in Australia by Capricorn Link (Australia) Pty. Ltd.
P.O. Box 704, Windsor, NSW 2756, Australia

Illustrations © Olga Axyutina/istock

Printed in China
All rights reserved

Sterling ISBN 978-1-4027-5791-4

For information about custom editions, special sales, premium and
corporate purchases, please contact Sterling Special Sales Department
at 800-805-5489 or specialsales@sterlingpublishing.com.

CONTENTS

To Osho

INTRODUCTION

The primary "rule" by which we have selected the
quotations in this book is governed by the need to inspire.
Unlike a political, literary, poetic, or humorous quotation,
the spiritual quotation has only one true motive in existing
beyond the mouth that spoke it or the hand that recorded
it—to make a connection with the divine, or inspire the
reader into some fundamental, internal change of view,
however small.

This rule can be applied, of course, across many different,
if not all, spiritual persuasions. There are no rules to this
rule—we are all quite different in what we find appealing and
inspiring, so the choice of words can be broad.

It is not that we can only choose quotations from religious
leaders; many hundreds of writers and speakers have found

ways of expressing the divine spirit without ever having enjoyed any formal or informal religious qualification. So the choice is wide.

The choices can also be made from virtually all ages of humanity. We can go back to Ancient Egypt or the *Upanishads*, the Sanskrit teachings that were composed nearly three thousand years ago in India, and find a plethora of material to inspire us. Or look into the origins of Sumeria which grew out of the city of Ur during the third millennium BCE.

Equally we can visit recent centuries and find as much power from the mouths of G. I. Gurdjieff, or Carlos Castaneda, Hermann Hesse, or D. H. Lawrence, the sole criterion being the presence of the soul criterion.

The book is arranged in themes, with each theme giving the authors in chronological order by birth date, or, in the case of quotations from works such as the Koran where there is no known author or several authors, approximate first publication dates. The thematic device is intended to help the reader indulge whatever particular aspect of the divine appeals, and the chronological order is designed to give a timeline of spiritual history and some idea of who lived during the same eras in different cultures and nations.

Some of the quotations, of course, are derived from sources that are "as old as the hills," so that it is not always possible to date them accurately, or indeed necessarily provide an author or source of any kind. But the vast majority of the quotations are sourced.

ANGELS

Philo of Alexandria (1st Century BCE)

Not only is it [the air] not alone deserted by all things besides, it is rather like a populous city, full of imperishable and immortal citizens, souls equal in number to the stars. Now regarding these souls, some descend upon the earth so as to be bound up in mortal bodies....Others soar upwards.... While others, condemning the body to be a great folly and trifling, have pronounced it a prison and a grave. Flying from it as from a house of correction or a tomb, they have raised themselves aloft on light wings toward the aether, devoting their whole lives to sublime speculations. Again there are others—the purest and most excellent of all—who possess greater and more divine intellects and never by any chance desire any earthly thing whatever, being, as it were, lieutenants of the Ruler of the universe, as though they were the eyes and ears of the great kings, behold and listen to everything. Philosophers in general are apt to call these demons, but the sacred scriptures call them angels, using a name more in accord with nature

ON DREAMS

New Testament
Be not forgetful to entertain strangers: for thereby some have entertained angels unawares.

HEBREWS 13:2

The Koran (7th Century)
Each has guardian angels before him and behind him, who watch him by God's command.

Saint Bridget of Sweden (1303-1373)
I beheld a Virgin of extreme beauty wrapped in a white mantle and a delicate tunic…with her beautiful golden hair falling loosely down her shoulders…. She stood with uplifted hands,

her eyes fixed on heaven, rapt, as it were, in an ecstasy of contemplation, in a rapture of divine sweetness. And while she stood in prayer, I beheld her Child move in her womb and…she brought forth her Son, from Whom such ineffable light and splendor radiated that the sun could not be compared to it…. And then I heard the wonderful singing of many angels.

BOOK OF QUESTIONS

Sir Francis Bacon (1561–1626)

The desire of power in excess caused the angels to fall; the desire of knowledge in excess caused man to fall; but in charity there is no excess, neither can angel or man come in danger by it.

ESSAYS

William Shakespeare (1564–1616)

I tell thee, churlish priest,
A ministering angel shall my sister be
When thou liest howling.

HAMLET, V, I, 242

Robert Burton (1577-1640)

Every man hath a good and a bad angel attending on him in
particular, all his life long.

ANATOMY OF MELANCHOLY

Blaise Pascal (1623-1662)

Man is neither angel or brute, and the unfortunate thing is
that he who would act the angel acts the brute.

PENSÉES

Joseph Addison (1672-1719)

If the notion of a gradual rise in Beings from the meanest to
the most High be not a vain imagination, it is not improbable
that an Angel looks down upon a Man, as Man doeth upon a
Creature which approaches the nearest to the rational Nature.

THE SPECTATOR, NOVEMBER 17, 1714

Alexander Pope (1688-1744)

Ambition . . . The glorious fault of angels and of gods.

ELEGY TO THE MEMORY OF AN UNFORTUNATE LADY

John Henry Newman (1801-1890)

On Thee the Angels look and are at peace; that is why they have perfect bliss. They never can lose their blessedness, for they never can lose Thee. They have no anxiety, no misgivings—because they love the Creator.

MEDITATIONS AND DEVOTIONS

Benjamin Disraeli (1804-1881)

What is the question now placed before society with the glib assurance which to me is most astonishing? That question is this: Is man an ape or an angel? I, my lord, I am on the side of the angels. I repudiate with indignation and abhorrence those newfangled theories.

SPEECH AT MEETING OF SOCIETY FOR INCREASING ENDOWMENTS OF SMALL LIVINGS IN THE DIOCESE OF OXFORD

Henry Ward Beecher (1813-1887)

There's not much practical Christianity in the man who lives on better terms with angels and seraphs, than with his children, servants, and neighbors.

ROYAL TRUTHS

Edwin Burne-Jones (1833-1898)

The more materialistic science becomes, the more angels shall I paint: Their wings are my protest in favor of the immortality of the soul.

TO OSCAR WILDE

Kahlil Gibran (1883-1931)

Only the naked live in the sun. Only the artless ride the wind. And he alone who loses his way a thousand times shall have a homecoming.

The angels are tired of the clever. And it was but yesterday that an angel said to me: "We created hell for those who glitter. What else but fire can erase a shining surface and melt a thing at its core?"

THE GARDEN OF THE PROPHET

Alan Watts (1915-1973)

It is high time to ask whether it is really any scandal, any deplorable inconsistency, for a human being to be both angel and animal with equal devotion…. Not to cherish both the angel and the animal, both the spirit and the flesh, is to renounce the whole interest and greatness of being human, and it is really tragic that those in whom the two natures are equally strong should be made to feel in conflict with themselves. For the saint-sinner and the mystic-sensualist is always the most interesting type of human being because he is the most complete. When the two aspects are seen to be consistent with each other, there is a real sense in which spirit transforms nature: that is to say, the animality of the mystic is always richer, more refined, and more subtly sensuous than the animality of the merely animal man.

THIS IS IT: AND OTHER ESSAYS ON ZEN AND SPIRITUAL EXPERIENCE

BEAUTY

Amenhotep IV (14th Century BCE)

Thy dawning is beautiful in the horizon of the sky,
O living Aton, Beginning of life!
When thou risest in the eastern horizon
Thou fillest every land with thy beauty.
Thou art beautiful, great, glittering, high above every land,
Thy rays, they encompass the lands, even all that thou
    hast made.

Though thou art far away, thy rays are upon earth;
Though thou art on high, thy footprints are the day.

HYMN TO ATON, THE CREATOR

Aristotle (384-322 BCE)

Beauty is the gift of God.

QUOTED IN DIOGENES LAËRTIUS,
LIVES OF EMINENT PHILOSOPHERS

Old Testament

He [God] hath made every thing beautiful in his time.

ECCLESIASTES 3:11

Plotinus (203-262)

Withdraw into yourself and look. And if you do not find
yourself beautiful yet, act as does the creator of a statue that
is to be made beautiful; he cuts away here, he smooths there,
he makes this line lighter, this other purer, until a lovely face
has grown upon his work. So do you also; cut away all that is
excessive, straighten all that is crooked, bring light to all that
is in shadow; labor to make all one glow of beauty and never
cease chiselling your statue until there shall shine out on you
from it the godlike splendor of virtue, until you shall see the
perfect Goodness established in the stainless shrine.

ENNEADS

Saint Augustine (354-430)

Too late I loved you, O Beauty so ancient yet ever new! Too late I loved you! And, behold, you were within me, and I out of myself, and there I searched for you.

CONFESSIONS, X, 27

Murasaki Shikibu (c. 974-1031)

Beauty without color seems somehow to belong to another world.

THE TALE OF GENJI

Jami (1414-1492)

Do not begrudge me my ugly exterior,
you who are lacking all virtue and fairness!
This body's a scabbard,
the soul is the sabre:
in the sabre is action
—not in the scabbard.

THE ABODE OF SPRING

Kabir (c. 1440–1518)

Do not go to the garden of flowers! O Friend! Go not there,
In your body is the garden of flowers.
Take your seat on the thousand petals of the lotus,
and there gaze on the Infinite Beauty.

ONE HUNDRED POEMS OF KABIR

Mira Bai (c. 1498–1546)

Having beheld Thy beauty
I am caught and enmeshed.
My family members repeatedly try to restrain me,
But attachment to the Dancer with the Peacock
    Plume [Krishna]
Has now sunk deep.

SONGS OF LOVE, DEVOTIONAL POEMS

William Shakespeare (1564–1616)

Beauty is a witch.

MUCH ADO ABOUT NOTHING, II, I, 177

O, she doth teach the torches to burn bright!
It seems she hangs upon the cheek of night
As a rich jewel in an Ethiop's ear—
Beauty too rich for use, for earth too dear!
ROMEO AND JULIET, I, V, 46

She speaks, yet she says nothing.
ROMEO AND JULIET, II, II, 12

From fairest creatures we desire increase,
That thereby beauty's rose might never die.
SONNET 1

The ornament of beauty is suspect.
SONNET 70

There's nothing ill can dwell in such a temple.
If the ill spirit have so fair a house,
Good things will strive to dwell with it.
THE TEMPEST, I, II, 458

Jacob Böhme (1575-1624)

Now observe: If thou fixest thy thoughts concerning heaven, and wouldst willingly conceive in thy mind what it is and where it is and how it is, thou needst not to cast thy thoughts many thousand miles off, for that place, that heaven [above in the sky], is not thy heaven.

And though indeed that is united with thy heaven as one body, and so together is but the one body of God, yet thou art not become a creature in that very place which is above many hundred thousand miles off, but thou art in the heaven of this world, which contains also in it such a Deep as is not of any human numbering.

The true heaven is everywhere, even in that very place where thou standest and goest; and so when thy spirit presses through the astral and the fleshly, and apprehends the inmost moving of God, then it is clearly in heaven.

But that there is assuredly a pure glorious heaven in all the three movings aloft above the deep of this world, in which God's Being together with that of the holy angels springs up very purely, brightly, beauteously, and joyfully, is undeniable. And he is not born of God that denies it.

THE CONFESSIONS

Marie de Sévigné (1626-1696)

There is nothing so lovely as to be beautiful. Beauty is a gift of God and we should cherish it as such.

LETTERS OF MADAME DE SÉVIGNÉ TO HER DAUGHTER AND FRIENDS

Yosa Buson (1715-1783)

In the rains of spring
An umbrella and raincoat
Pass by, conversing.

HAIKU

John Keats (1795-1821)

Beauty is truth, truth beauty—that is all Ye know on earth, and all ye need to know.

ODE ON A GRECIAN URN

A thing of beauty is a joy for ever;
Its loveliness increases; it will never
Pass into nothingness; but still will keep
A bower quiet for us, and a sleep
Full of sweet dreams, and health,
and quiet breathing.

ENDYMION

John Ruskin (1819-1900)

Remember that the most beautiful things in the world are the
most useless: peacocks and lilies, for instance.

THE STONES OF VENICE

Charles Baudelaire (1821-1867)

What do I care if you are good? Be beautiful! and be sad!

"MADRIGAL TRISTE," IN *NOUVELLES FLEURS DU MAL*

Leo Tolstoy (1828-1910)

It is amazing how complete is the delusion that beauty
is goodness.

THE KREUTZER SONATA

William McCall (1870-1938)

Straight is the line of duty;
Curved is the line of beauty;
Follow the straight line, thou shalt see
The curved line ever follow thee.

UNTITLED

Robert Bridges (1844-1930)

For beauty being the best of all we know
Sums up the unsearchable and secret aims
Of nature.

THE GROWTH OF LOVE

Gerard Manley Hopkins (1844-1889)

Come then, your ways and airs and looks, locks, maiden gear,
    gallantry and gaiety and grace,
Winning ways, airs innocent, maiden manners, sweet looks,
    loose locks, long locks, lovelocks, gaygear, going gallant,
    girl-grace—

Resign them, sign them, seal them, send them, motion them
   with breath,
And with sighs soaring, soaring sighs deliver
Them; beauty-in-the-ghost, deliver it, early now, long
   before death
Give beauty back, beauty, beauty, beauty, back to God,
   beauty's self and beauty's giver.
THE LEADEN ECHO AND THE GOLDEN ECHO

Margaret Hungerford (1855-1897)
Beauty is in the eye of the beholder.
MOLLY BAWN

Thorstein Veblen (1857-1929)
The superior gratification derived from the use and
contemplation of costly and supposedly beautiful products is,
commonly, in great measure, a gratification of our sense of
costliness masquerading under the name of beauty.
THE THEORY OF THE LEISURE CLASS

G. K. Chesterton (1874-1936)

Every true artist does feel, consciously or unconsciously, that he is touching transcendental truths; that his images are shadows of things seen through the veil. In other words, the natural mystic does know that there is something *there*; something behind the clouds or within the trees; but he believes that the pursuit of beauty is the way to find it; that imagination is a sort of incantation that can call it up.

THE EVERLASTING MAN

Isadora Duncan (1878-1927)

The artist is the only lover, he alone has the pure vision of beauty, and love is the vision of the soul when it is permitted to gaze upon immortal beauty.

MY LIFE

Hazrat Inayat Khan (1882-1927)

The purpose of creation is beauty. Nature in all its various aspects develops toward beauty, and therefore it is plain that the purpose of life is to evolve toward beauty.

THE SUFI MESSAGE OF HAZRAT INAYAT KHAN:
THE ART OF PERSONALITY

Virginia Woolf (1882-1941)

The beauty of the world which is soon to perish, has two edges, one of laughter, one of anguish, cutting the heart asunder.

A ROOM OF ONE'S OWN

D. H. Lawrence (1885-1930)

Sex and beauty are inseparable, like life and consciousness.

SEX VERSUS LONELINESS

Marianne Moore (1887-1972)

Beauty is everlasting
And dust is for a time.

IN DISTRUST OF MERITS

Dorothy Parker (1893-1967)

I might repeat to myself, slowly and soothingly,
a list of quotations beautiful from minds profound;
if I can remember any of the damn things.

THE LITTLE HOURS

Dylan Thomas (1914-1953)

Light breaks on secret lots…
Where logics die
The secret grows through the eye.

UNTITLED

Anne Frank (1929-1945)

Think of all the beauty still left around you and be happy.

DIARY OF A YOUNG GIRL

Osho (1931-1990)

Whenever you say, "This is beautiful," you have brought ugliness into the world. Don't you see. Whenever you say, "I love," you have brought hatred into the world. Whenever you say, "You are my friend," you have brought enmity into the world. Whenever you say, "This is good, right, moral," you have brought immorality into the world, you have brought the devil into the world. In deep silence, when you don't know what is good and what is bad, you don't utter any labels and names, in that silence the duality disappears, the split disappears. The world becomes one.

DISCOURSES

Jean Kerr (Contemporary)

I'm tired of all this business about beauty being only skin-deep.
That's deep enough. What do you want—an adorable pancreas?

"MIRROR, MIRROR ON THE WALL," IN *THE SNAKE HAS ALL THE LINES*

BELIEF
AND DOUBT

Lao Tzu (c. 6th Century BCE)

When the highest type of men hear Tao,
They diligently practice it.
When the average type of men hear Tao,
They half believe in it.
When the lowest type of men hear Tao,
They laugh heartily at it.

TAO TE CHING

The Tao that can be told of is not the eternal Tao;
The name that can be named is not the eternal name.
The Nameless is the origin of Heaven and Earth;
The Named is the mother of all things.
Therefore let there always be non-being, so we may see
    their subtlety,
And let there always be being, so we may see their outcome.
The two are the same,
But after they are produced, they have different names.
They both may be called deep and profound.
Deeper and more profound,
The door of all subtleties.

TAO TE CHING

Confucius (551-479 BCE)

Confucius said, "When you see a good man, try to emulate
his example, and when you see a bad man, search yourself for
his faults."

THE APHORISMS OF CONFUCIUS, V, "WIT AND WISDOM"

The Bhagavad Gita (c. 500 BCE)

Man is made by his belief. As he believes, so he is.

Chuang Tzu (369-286 BCE)

Granting that you and I argue. If you get the better of me,
and not I of you, are you necessarily right and I wrong? Or
if I get the better of you and not you of me, am I necessarily
right and you wrong? Or are we both partly right and partly
wrong? Or are we both wholly right and wholly wrong? You
and I cannot know this, and consequently we all live
in darkness.

ON LEVELING ALL THINGS

Asoka (c. 269-232 BCE)

It is forbidden to descry other sects; the true believer gives
honor to whatever in them is worthy of honor.

EDICTS

Saint John Climacus (525-600)

Faith furnishes prayer with wings, without which it cannot soar to Heaven.

THE LADDER OF DIVINE ASCENT

Medieval Latin Saying

Believe, that you may understand.

Peter Abelard (1079-1142)

The first key to wisdom is assiduous and frequent questioning.... For by doubting we come to inquiry, and by inquiry we arrive at truth.

THEOLOGIA

Hakim Sanai (12th Century)

The head has two ears;
love [of God] has just one:
this hears certitude,
whilst those hear doubt.

THE WALLED GARDEN OF TRUTH

Farid ud-Din Attar (c. 1120-1193)

If disappointments darken all your days,
You need not grieve, for nothing worldly stays—
It is your passion for magnificence
That prompts your tears, not fancied indigence.

THE CONFERENCE OF THE BIRDS

Jalal al-Din Rumi (1207-1273)

The wisdom of this world increases surmise and doubt; the
wisdom of true religion soars beyond the sky.

TALES OF THE MASNAVI

I have put duality away, I have seen that the two worlds are
one: one I seek, one I know, one I see, one I call. He is the
first, he is the last. He is the outward, he is the inward.

TALES OF THE MASNAVI

Sir Francis Bacon (1561-1626)

Give to faith the things which belong to faith.

ADVANCEMENT OF LEARNING

René Descartes (1596-1650)

If you would be a real seeker after truth, it is necessary that at least once in your life you doubt, as far as possible, all things.
PRINCIPLES OF PHILOSOPHY

Sir Thomas Browne (1605-1682)

To believe only possibilities is not Faith, but mere Philosophy.
RELIGIO MEDICI

John Milton (1608-1674)

A man may be heretic in the truth if he believes things only because his pastor says so, or the assembly so determines, without knowing other reason; though his belief be true, yet the very truth he holds becomes his heresy.
AREOPAGITICA

Molière (1622-1673)

Doubts are more cruel than the worst of truths.
THE MISANTHROPE

Blaise Pascal (1623-1662)

It is your own assent to yourself, and the constant voice of your own reason, and not of others, that should make you believe.

PENSÉES

Samuel Johnson (1709-1784)

Every man who attacks my belief diminishes in some degree my confidence in it, and therefore makes me uneasy, and I am angry with him who makes me uneasy.

QUOTED IN *LIFE OF JOHNSON*, JAMES BOSWELL

William Cowper (1731-1800)

Each man's belief is right in his own eyes.

HOPE

J. W. von Goethe (1749-1832)

I believe in God—this is a fine, praise-worthy thing to say. But to acknowledge God wherever and however He manifest Himself, that in truth is heavenly bliss on earth.

MAXIMS AND REFLECTIONS

Give me the benefit of your convictions, if you have any, but keep your doubts to yourself, for I have enough of my own.

MAXIMS AND REFLECTIONS

William Blake (1757-1827)

Every thing possible to be believ'd is an image of truth.
He who doubts from what he sees
Will ne'er believe, do what you please.
If the sun and moon should doubt,
They'd immediately go out.

AUGURIES OF INNOCENCE

Napoleon Bonaparte (1791-1821)

All the scholastic scaffolding falls, as a ruined edifice, before one single word—faith.

LETTER TO COUNT THIBAUDEAU, JUNE 6, 1801

John Keats (1795-1821)

I am certain of nothing but of the holiness of the heart's affections, and the truth of the Imagination.

LETTER, NOVEMBER 22, 1817

John Henry Newman (1801-1890)

It is as absurd to argue men, as to torture them, into believing.

APOLOGIA PRO VITA SUA

Jean Baptiste Lacordaire (1802-1861)

What takes place in us when we believe is a phenomenon of intimate and superhuman light.

CONFERENCES DE NOTRE DAME DE PARIS, 17TH CONFERENCE, 1850

W. Bernard Ullathorne (1806-1889)

Nothing in this world is so marvelous as the transformation that a soul undergoes when the light of faith descends upon the light of reason.

FROM CABIN-BOY TO ARCHBISHOP

Robert Browning (1812-1889)

Who knows most, doubts most.

MOTTO

Søren Kierkegaard (1813-1855)

The method which begins by doubting in order to
philosophize is just as suited to its purpose as making
a soldier lie down in a heap in order to teach him to
stand up straight.

LIFE

Walt Whitman (1819-1892)

Of the terrible doubt of appearances,
Of the uncertainly after all, that we may be deluded,
That may-be reliance and hope are but speculations after all,
That may-be identity beyond the grave is a beautiful
     fable only....

OF THE TERRIBLE DOUBT OF APPEARANCES

James Russell Lowell (1819-1891)

Toward no crimes have men shown themselves so cold-
bloodedly cruel as in punishing differences in belief.

WITCHCRAFT, VOL. 2

Henri Frédéric Amiel (1821–1881)

A belief is not true because it is useful.

JOURNAL

Fyodor Dostoevsky (1821–1881)

Believe to the end, even if all men went astray and you were
left the only one faithful; bring your offering even then and
praise God in your loneliness.

THE BROTHERS KARAMAZOV

Thomas Henry Huxley (1825–1895)

What we call rational grounds for our beliefs are often
extremely irrational attempts to justify our instincts.

ON THE NATURAL INEQUALITY OF MAN

Shivapuri Baba (1826–1963)

If you believe in God, then your search must be for God;
but even if you believe in nothing, you must still have some
conviction that there is a meaning behind the visible world. You
must be determined to seek out that meaning and understand it.

QUOTED IN *LONG PILGRIMAGE*, J. G. BENNETT

Henry George (1839-1897)

In this tendency to accept what we find, to believe what we are told, is at once good and evil. It is this which makes social advance possible; it is this which makes it so slow and painful. It is thus tyranny is maintained and superstition perpetuated.

SOCIAL PROBLEMS

Oscar Wilde (1854-1900)

Man can believe the impossible, but man can never believe the improbable.

THE DECAY OF LIVING

Harry Emerson Fosdick (1878-1969)

It is cynicism and fear that freeze life; it is faith that thaws it out, releases it, sets it free.

THE HOPE OF THE WORLD

H. L. Mencken (1880-1956)

Faith may be defined briefly as an illogical belief in the occurrence of the improbable.

PREJUDICES

Kahlil Gibran (1883–1931)

Doubt is a pain too lonely to know that faith is his
   twin brother.
Doubt is a foundling unhappy and astray, and though his
   own mother who gave him birth should find him and
   enfold him, he would withdraw in caution and in fear.

*JESUS: THE SON OF MAN: HIS WORDS AND HIS DEEDS
AS TOLD AND RECORDED BY THOSE WHO KNEW HIM*

François Mauriac (1885–1970)

Doubt is nothing but a trivial agitation on the surface of the
soul, while deep down there is a calm certainty.

GOD AND MAMMON

Walter Lippman (1889–1974)

Many a time I have wanted to stop talking and find out what
I really believed.

OBSERVER, MARCH 27, 1938

J. Krishnamurti (1895-1986)

The constant assertion of belief is an indication of fear.

THE SECOND PENGUIN KRISHNAMURTI READER

Alan Watts (1915-1973)

The attitude of faith must be basic—the final and fundamental attitude—and the attitude of doubt secondary and subordinate. This is another way of saying that toward the vast and all-encompassing background of human life, with which the philosopher as artist is concerned, there must be total affirmation and acceptance. Otherwise there is no basis at all for caution and control with respect to details in the foreground. But it is all too easy to become so absorbed in these details that all sense of proportion is lost, and for man to make himself mad by trying to bring everything under his control. We become insane, unsound, and without foundation when we lose consciousness of and faith in the uncontrolled and ungraspable background world which is ultimately what we ourselves are. And there is a very slight distinction, if any, between complete, conscious faith and love.

THIS IS IT: AND OTHER ESSAYS ON ZEN AND SPIRITUAL EXPERIENCE

You know that if you get in the water and have nothing to hold on to, but try to behave as you would on dry land, you will drown. But if, on the other hand, you trust yourself to the water and let go, you will float. And this is exactly the situation of faith.

THE WAY OF LIBERATION

Osho (1931–1990)

Your personalities are nothing but dolls tied to your feet. I don't have to know your personal life, your personality. I don't have to be acquainted with you personally, I know you essentially. By knowing myself, I have known you all. By dissolving my own problems I know your problems, and I know the key to how they can be dissolved.

DISCOURSES

Deepak Chopra (Contemporary)

To find oneself living in an age of doubt is not such a curse.
There is a kind of reverence in undertaking the quest for
truth, even before the first scrap has been found.

UNCONDITIONAL LIFE

Theodore M. Hesburgh (Contemporary)

Faith is not an easy virtue but in the broad world of man's
total voyage through time to eternity, faith is not only a
gracious companion, but an essential guide.

THE WAY, JUNE 1963

Carter Heywood (Contemporary)

But doubt is as crucial to faith as darkness is to light. Without
one, the other has no context and is meaningless. Faith is, by
definition, uncertainty. It is full of doubt, steeped in risk. It is
about matters not of the known, but of the unknown.

A PRIEST FOREVER

U. G. Krishnamurti (Contemporary)

Your situation and prospects only seem hopeless because you have ideas of hope; knock off that hope and the crippling feelings of helplessness go with it. There is bound to be helplessness and overwhelming frustration as long as you exist in relationship with the hope for fulfilment, because there is no fulfilment at all.

MIND IS A MYTH — DISQUIETING CONVERSATIONS WITH A MAN CALLED U. G.

THE BODY

Proverb

If thine eye be single, thy whole body shall be full of light.

Lao Tzu (c. 6th Century BCE)

A journey of a thousand miles must begin with a single step.

The softest things in the world overcome the hardest things
in the world.

Non-being penetrates that in which there is no space.

Through this I know the advantage of taking no action.

One may know the world without going out of doors.

One may see the way of Heaven without looking through
the windows.

The further one goes, the less one knows.

Therefore the sage knows without going about,

Understands without seeing,
And accomplishes without any action.

TAO TE CHING

The Bhagavad Gita (c. 500 BCE)

These bodies are perishable; but the dwellers in these bodies
are eternal, indestructible, and impenetrable.

Mencius (372-289 BCE)

Is it only the mouth and belly which are injured by hunger
and thirst? Men's minds are also injured by them.

BOOK VII

Epictetus (55-135)

It is more necessary for the soul to be healed than the body;
for it is better to die than to live ill.

DISCOURSES

He whose body is chained, and his soul unbound, is free.

DISCOURSES

Juvenal (65-127)

Our prayers should be for a sound mind in a healthy body.

THE SATIRES

Petronius (c. 27-66)

From a man's face, I can read his character; if I can see him walk, I know his thoughts.

SATYRICON

Shankara (788-820)

You never identify yourself with the shadow cast by your body, or with its reflection, or with the body you see in a dream or in your imagination. Therefore you should not identify yourself with this living body, either.

CREST-JEWEL OF DISCRIMINATION

One's body may be handsome, wife beautiful, fame excellent and varied, and wealth like unto Mount Meru; but if one's mind be not attached to the lotus feet of the *Guru* [teacher], what thence, what thence, what thence, what thence?

THE HYMNS OF SHANKARA

Let there be births as a human being, as a god, as a mountain, or forest-animal, as a mosquito, cow or worm, as a bird or as any other. If the heart, here, is ever given to sporting in the flood of supreme bliss consisting of the contemplation of Thy lotus-feet, what does it matter in which body one is born?

SIVANANDALAHARI

Jalal al-Din Rumi (1207-1273)

Know then that a fine and handsome exterior when paired with a bad character is not worth a sou; whereas if the exterior is unpleasing and contemptible but the disposition is good, you may gladly die at such a person's feet. Know that the external form passes away, whereas the world of inner truth abides eternally.

TALES OF THE MASNAVI

God's wisdom in manifesting the world...is that which was known should come forth visibly. Until He made visible that which He knew, He did not impose upon the world the pains and throes of delivery. Not for a single moment can you sit inactive, without some evil or goodness issuing from you.

These cravings for action were committed to you so that your secret heart might become visible. How should the reel, the body, ever be at rest seeing that the end of the thread, the mind, is always tugging it? The token of that tugging is your restlessness; to be inactive is for you like the agony of death. This world and the world beyond are forever giving birth; every cause is a mother, whereof the effect is the child. As soon as the effect is born it becomes a cause, so that other marvelous effects may be born of it. These causes mount back generation on generation, but it requires a very illumined eye to see the links.

TALES OF THE MASNAVI

Michel de Montaigne (1533-1592)

Good looks are a possession of great value in human relations; they are the first means of establishing goodwill between men, and no one can be so barbarous or so surly as not to feel their attraction in some degree. The body enjoys a great share in our being, and has an eminent place in it. Its structure and composition, therefore, are worthy of proper consideration.

ESSAYS

Those who would divide our two principal parts, and isolate one from the other, are in the wrong. On the contrary, we must reunite them and bring them together. We must command the soul not to draw aside and hold herself apart, not to scorn and abandon the body—which she can only do by some false pretense—but to ally herself with it, help control, advise, and correct it, and bring it back when it goes astray; in short, marry it and become its partner, so that their actions may not appear diverse and opposed, but harmonious and uniform. Christians have some particular instruction concerning this bond. For they know that divine justice embraces the union and fellowship of body and soul, to the extent of making the body capable of eternal rewards; and that God regards the actions of the whole man, and wills him to receive as a whole his punishment or reward according to this deserts.

ESSAYS

I, who am a very earthy person, loathe that inhuman teaching which would make us despise and dislike the care of the body. I consider it just as wrong to reject natural pleasures as to set too much store by them.

ESSAYS

Our great, divine, and heavenly King, about whom every detail should be carefully, religiously, and reverently noticed, did not despise bodily superiority, for He was "fairer than the children of men" [Psalms, 45, 2]. And Plato desires beauty, as well as temperance and courage, in the guardians of his Republic.

ESSAYS

We are all convention; convention carries us away, and we neglect the substance of things. We hold on to the branches, and let go the trunk and the body. We have taught ladies to blush at the mere mention of things they are not in the least afraid to do. We dare not call our parts by their right names, but are not afraid to use them for every sort of debauchery.

Convention forbids us to express in words things that are lawful and natural; and we obey it. Reason forbids us to do what is unlawful or wicked, and no one obeys it.

ESSAYS

William Shakespeare (1564-1616)

I have more flesh than another man, and therefore more frailty.

HENRY IV, PART I, III, III

John Donne (1572-1631)

Love's mysteries in souls do grow,
But yet the body is his book.

THE ECSTASY

Izaak Walton (1593-1683)

Look to your health; and if you have it, praise God, and value it next to a good conscience; for health is the second blessing that we mortals are capable of; a blessing that money cannot buy.

COMPLEAT ANGLER

James Thomson (1700-1748)

But what avail the largest gifts of Heaven,
When drooping health and spirits go amiss?
How tasteless then whatever can be given!
Health is the vital principle of bliss.

CASTLE OF INDOLENCE

Henry Wadsworth Longfellow (1807-1882)

How wonderful is the human voice! It is indeed the organ of the soul! The intellect of man sits enthroned visibly upon the forehead and in his eye; and the heart of man is written upon his countenance. But the soul reveals itself in the voice only, as God revealed himself to the prophet of old, in the "still, small voice," and in a voice from the burning bush.

The soul of man is audible, not visible. A sound alone betrays the flowing of the eternal fountain, invisible to man!

QUOTED IN ELBERT HUBBARD'S SCRAPBOOK, BY ELBERT HUBBARD

Walt Whitman (1819-1892)

If anything is sacred the human body is sacred.

I SING THE BODY ELECTRIC

I sing the body electric,
The armies of those I love engirth me and I engirth them,
They will not let me off till I go with them, respond to them,
And discorrupt them, and charge them full with the charge
   of the soul.

I SING THE BODY ELECTRIC

Shivapuri Baba (1826-1963)

Now, unless you live a disciplined life, this meditation
is not possible. There is this body; you should know the
requirements of this body. You will have to hear, you will have
to see, you will have to sleep, you will have to taste, you will
have to spit, you will have to breathe. One thousand activities
are there in this body. All these activities are to be controlled
and commanded. How much to eat, how much to sleep,

what to see, what to hear? All this should be controlled and commanded. This is one duty.

Another duty is toward home, society, nation, etc. Find out what we have to do.

QUOTED IN *LONG PILGRIMAGE*, J. G. BENNETT

Margaret Oliphant (1828-1897)

The first thing which I can record concerning myself is, that I was born…. These are wonderful words. This life, to which neither time nor eternity can bring diminution—this everlasting living soul, *began*. My mind loses itself in these depths.

MEMOIRS AND RESOLUTIONS OF ADAM GRAEME, OF MOSSGRAY

Leo Tolstoy (1828-1910)

A religious man is guided in his activity not by the consequences of his action, but by the consciousness of the destination of his life.

CONFESSIONS

Friedrich Wilhelm Nietzsche (1844-1900)

Great health—a health such as one does not merely have but has continually to win because one has again and again to sacrifice it.

ECCE HOMO

George Santayana (1863-1952)

For how are we to conceive that preexisting consciousness should govern the formation of the body, move, warm, or guide it?

THE LIFE OF REASON

G. I. Gurdjieff (c. 1877-1949)

The sole means now for the saving of beings of the planet Earth would be to implant again into their presences a new organ... of such properties that every one of these unfortunates during the process of existence should constantly sense and be cognizant of the inevitability of his own death as well as the death of everyone upon whom

his eyes or attention rests. Only such a sensation and
such a cognizance can now destroy the egoism completely
crystallized in them.
ALL AND EVERYTHING

The Mother (1878-1973)

If you want to experience the body, you must live in the body!
That's why the ancient sages and saints didn't know what to
do with their body: They left it and they meditated, so the
body didn't participate at all.
SATPREM, *THE MIND OF THE CELLS*

What the body is learning is this: to replace the mental
rule of intelligence by the spiritual rule of consciousness
(the other state). And that makes a tremendous difference
(although it doesn't look like much, you can't notice
anything), to the point that it increases the body's
capabilities a hundredfold. When the body follows certain
rules, however broad they may be, it is a slave to those

rules, and its possibilities are limited accordingly. But
when it is governed by the spirit and consciousness
(of the other state) its possibilities and flexibility become
exceptional! And that's how it will acquire the capacity
to extend its life at will.

SATPREM, *THE MIND OF THE CELLS*

Mabel Dodge Luhan (1879-1962)

The strongest, surest way to the soul is through the flesh.

LORENZO IN TAOS

D. H. Lawrence (1885-1930)

My great religion is a belief in the blood, the flesh, as being
wiser than the intellect. We can go wrong in our minds. But
what our blood feels and believes and says, is always true.

LETTER TO ERNEST COLLINS, JANUARY 17, 1913,
COLLECTED LETTERS OF D. H. LAWRENCE

Mikhail Naimy (1889-1988)

Your breath upon the wind shall surely lodge within some breast. Ask not whose breast it is. See only that the breath itself be pure.

THE BOOK OF MIRDAD—A LIGHTHOUSE AND A HAVEN

Martha Graham (1894-1991)

The body says what words cannot.

INTERVIEW, THE NEW YORK TIMES, MARCH 31, 1985

Louise Bogan (1897-1970)

O remember
In your narrow dark hours
That more things move
Than blood in the heart.

UNTITLED

Albert Camus (1913-1960)

Alas, after a certain age, every man is responsible for his own face.

THE FALL

Alan Watts (1915-1973)

Consider…that all your five senses are differing forms of one basic sense—something like touch. Seeing is highly sensitive touching. The eyes touch, or feel, light waves and so enable us to touch things out of reach of our hands. Similarly, the ears touch sound waves in the air, and the nose tiny particles of dust and gas.

THE BOOK: ON THE TABOO AGAINST KNOWING WHO YOU ARE

Osho (1931-1990)

The body has to be looked after: One has to be very caring about the body and very loving to the body. And then, its very spontaneity purifies it, makes it holy.

DISCOURSES

Da Free John (1839-2008)

If the design of man is examined he is revealed to be a composite of all previous creatures, environments, and experiences. His body below the brows is a machine of animals and elemental cycles.... He is not truly unique below the brows. He is rather a summation of all that came before him and everything he already knows. But man is also a new stage in the event of time. His newness or uniqueness is hidden in the brain. His lower, or vital, brain, including his rudimentary speech and thought, is part of the summary and reflection of the past.

THE ENLIGHTENMENT OF THE WHOLE BODY

Jamake Highwater (c. 1930-2001)

"But here," Patu murmured, grazing at her fingers, "here in the skin of our fingertips we see the trail of the wind." And then she made a circular motion to indicate the whirlwind that had left its imprint in the whorl at the tips of the human finger. "It shows where the wind blew life into my ancestors when they were first made. It was in the legend days when these lines happened. It was in the legend days when the first people were given the breath of life."

QUOTED IN NATIVE AMERICAN WISDOM

U. G. Krishnamurti (Contemporary)

The body is affected by everything that is happening around you; it is not separate from what is happening around you. Whatever is happening there, is also happening here—there is only the physical response. This is affection.

CONVERSATIONS WITH A MAN CALLED U. G.

Idris Parry (1916-2008)

What evidence is there that the five senses, taken together, do cover the whole of possible existence? They cover simply our actual experience, our human knowledge of facts and events. There are gaps between the fingers; there are gaps between the senses. In these gaps is the darkness which hides the connection between things.... This darkness is the source of our vague fears and anxieties, but also the home of our gods. They alone see the connections, the total relevance of everything that happens; that which now comes to us in bits and pieces, the "accidents" which exist only in our heads, in our limited perceptions.

"KAFKA, RILKE AND RUMPELSTILTSKIN,"
ON *THE LISTENER*, BBC, DEC 2, 1965

Paul Jordan-Smith (c. 1900–1971)

It happened once that a group of physicians were in their cups and had fallen to quarreling about which part of the body was most important for life. As they could not agree among themselves, they decided to consult the rabbi.

"Of course it is the heart and blood vessels that are most important," said the first physician, "for on them the whole life of a man depends."

"Not at all," said the second physician. "It is the brain and nerves which are most vital, for without them, even the heart would not beat."

The third physician said, "You are both wrong. It is the stomach and the digestive passages which are important, for without the proper digestion of food, the body will die."

"The lungs are most important," declared the fourth, "for a man without air will surely die."

"You are all wrong," said the rabbi. "There are two vessels of the body only that are important, but you have no knowledge of them."

"What are they, then?" asked the physicians.

The rabbi replied, "The channel that runs from the ear to the soul, and the one that runs from the soul to the tongue."

ADAPTATION FROM *PARABOLA*, VOL. 3

Alice Walker (Contemporary)

The inner voice—the human compulsion when deeply distressed to seek healing counsel within ourselves, and the capacity within ourselves both to create this counsel and to receive it.

YOU CAN'T KEEP A GOOD WOMAN DOWN

CHILDREN
AND YOUTH

Mencius (372-289 BCE)

Mencius said, "All men have a mind which cannot bear (to see the sufferings of) others…. The ground on which I say [this] is this: Even nowadays, when men suddenly see a child about to fall into a well, they will all experience a feeling of alarm and distress. They will feel so not that they may gain the favor or the child's parents; nor that they may seek the praise of their neighbors and friends; nor from a dislike to the reputation of (being unmoved by) such a thing…. That feeling of distress is the principle of benevolence; the feeling of shame and dislike is the principle of righteousness; the feeling of modesty and complaisance is the principle of propriety; and the feeling of approving and disapproving is the principle of knowledge.

Men have these four principles just as they have their four limbs.

BOOK I

A great man is one who has not lost the child's heart.

BOOK I

Virgil (70-19 BCE)

Your descendants shall gather your fruits.

ECLOGUES

Shankara (788-820)

It is hard for any living creature to achieve birth in a human form.

CREST-JEWEL OF DISCRIMINATION

William Wordsworth (1770-1850)

My heart leaps up when I behold
A rainbow in the sky:
So was it when my life began;
So is it now I am a man;
So be it when I shall grow old,
Or let me die!
The Child is father of the Man;
And I could wish my days to be
Bound each to each by natural piety.

MY HEART LEAPS

Percy Bysshe Shelley (1792-1822)

Know ye what it is to be a child?… It is to have a spirit yet
streaming from the waters of baptism; it is to believe in love,
to believe in loveliness, to believe in belief.

LETTERS

Harriet Beecher Stowe (1811-1896)

"Do you know who made you?"

"Nobody, as I knows on," said the child, with a short laugh.
The idea appeared to amuse her considerably; for her eyes
twinkled, and she added—

"I 'spect I grow'd. Don't think nobody never made me."

UNCLE TOM'S CABIN

H. P. Blavatsky (1831-1891)

Can you remember what you were or did when a baby? Have
you preserved the smallest recollection of your life, thoughts,
or deeds, or that you lived at all during the first eighteen
months or two years of your existence?

THE KEY TO THEOSOPHY

Oscar Wilde (1854-1900)

Children begin by loving their parents; after a time they judge
them; rarely, if ever, do they forgive them.

A WOMAN OF NO IMPORTANCE

Rabindranath Tagore (1861-1941)

The child who is decked with prince's robes and who has jewelled chains round his neck loses all pleasure in his play; his dress hampers him at every step.

In fear that it may be frayed, or stained with dust he keeps himself from the world, and is afraid ever to move.

Mother, it is no gain, thy bondage of finery, if it keep one shut off from the healthful dust of the earth, if it rob one of the right of entrance to the great fair of common human life.

GITANJALI (SONG OFFERING)

Hazrat Inayat Khan (1882-1927)

The soul of an infant is like a photographic plate which has never been exposed before, and whatever impression falls on that photographic plate covers it; no other impressions which come afterward have the same effect.

THE SUFI MESSAGE OF HAZRAT INAYAT KHAN:
THE ART OF PERSONALITY

The soul that has come from above is received and is reared and taken care of by the mother; and therefore the mother is its best friend. If there is anything that the father can do, it is to help the mother or the guardian to educate the child. If the child in its infancy were given entirely into the hand of the father, there would be little hope that it would come out right; because a man is a child all his life, and the help that is needed in the life of an infant is that of the mother. Nevertheless, later in the life of a child there comes a time when the father's influence is equally needed; but that time is not in infancy. As the Brahmin says, the first Guru is the mother, the second Guru is the father, and the third Guru is the teacher.

THE SUFI MESSAGE OF HAZRAT INAYAT KHAN:
THE ART OF PERSONALITY

It is the will that has brought the child to the earth, otherwise it would not have come. It comes by its own will and it stays by its own will. The will is like the steam that makes the engine go forward. If the child wishes to go back, that depends upon its wish. It is always by the will of the soul. And therefore in the child you see the will in the form in which it has come. But often during childhood the will is broken, and then it remains broken all through life. If in childhood the parents took good care that the will was not broken, then the will would manifest itself in wonders. The child would do wonderful things in life if its will was sustained, if it was cherished.

THE SUFI MESSAGE OF HAZRAT INAYAT KHAN:
THE ART OF PERSONALITY

Kahlil Gibran (1883-1931)

And a woman who held a babe against her bosom said,
Speak to us of Children.
And he said:
Your children are not your children,
They are the sons and daughters of Life's longing for itself.
They come through you but not from you,

And though they are with you, yet they belong not to you.
You may give them your love but not your thoughts.
For they have their own thoughts.
You may house their bodies but not their souls,
For their souls dwell in the house of tomorrow,
which you cannot visit, not even in your dreams.
You may strive to be like them, but seek not
to make them like you.
For life goes not backward nor tarries with yesterday.
You are the bows from which your children
as living arrows are sent forth.
The archer sees the mark upon the path of the infinite,
and He bends you with His might
that His arrows may go swift and far.
Let your bending in the archer's hand be for gladness;
For even as he loves the arrow that flies,
so He loves the bow that is stable.

THE PROPHET

Osho (1931-1990)

The innocence of the child is his wisdom, the simplicity of the child is his egolessness. The freshness of the child is the freshness of your consciousness, which never becomes old, which always remains young.

DISCOURSES

Robert Bly (Contemporary)

Our own father, through his cowardice or fears, may have arranged our disasters before we were born.

IRON JOHN

Carlos Castaneda (1925-1998)

The fact of the matter is that many children *see*.... Most of those who *see* are considered to be oddballs and every effort is made to correct them.

THE FIRE WITHIN

Da Free John (1939-2008)

As a baby I remember crawling around inquisitively with an incredible sense of joy, light, and freedom in the middle of my head that was bathed in energies moving freely down from above, up, around, and down through my body and my heart. It was an expanding sphere of joy from the heart. And I was a radiant form, a source of energy, bliss, and light. And I was the power of Reality, a direct enjoyment and communication. I was the Heart, who lightens the mind and all things. I was the same as everyone and everything, except it became clear that others were unaware of the thing itself.

THE ENLIGHTENMENT OF THE WHOLE BODY

CONSCIOUSNESS

The Upanishads (c. 900-600 BCE)

It is not outer awareness
It is not inner awareness
Nor is it suspension of awareness
It is not knowing
It is not unknowing
Nor is it knowingness itself
It can neither be seen nor understood
It cannot be given boundaries
It is ineffable and beyond thought
It is indefinable
It is known only through becoming it.

MANDUKYA UPANISHAD

Shankara (788-820)

Who is thy wife? Who is thy son?
The ways of this world are strange indeed.
Whose art thou? When art thou come?
Vast is thy ignorance, my beloved.
Therefore ponder these things and worship the Lord.

THE SHATTERING OF ILLUSION

A clear vision of Reality may be obtained only through our own eyes, when they have been opened by spiritual insight—never through the eyes of some other seer. Through our own eyes we learn what the moon looks like: How could we learn this through the eyes of others?

CREST-JEWEL OF DISCRIMINATION

I am the soul of the universe. I am all things, and above all things. I am one without a second. I am pure consciousness, single and universal. I am joy. I am life everlasting.

CREST-JEWEL OF DISCRIMINATION

Judah ben Samuel (12th century)

One must beware of saying what he does not mean; instead
he must speak what is in his heart—one must match
his speech with what he believes. One must not deceive
anyone.... Even a single word of deception is forbidden.

SEFER HASIDIM

Jalal al-Din Rumi (1207-1273)

When you have seen your own cunning,
follow it back to its origin.
What is below comes from above.
Come on, turn your eyes to the heights.

TALES OF THE MATHNAWI

Know that every bad habit is a thornbush.
After all, how often have you stepped on its thorns?

TALES OF THE MATHNAWI

Learn to recognize the false dawn from the true; distinguish the color of the wine from the color of the cup. Then it may be that patience and time may produce, out of the spectrum-viewing sight, true vision, and you will behold colors other than these mortal hues, you will see pearls instead of stones. Pearls, did I say? Nay more, you will become a sea, you will become a sun traveling the sky.

TALES OF THE MASNAVI

John Keats (1795-1821)

When I have fears that I may cease to be
Before my pen has glean'd my teeming brain,
Before high-piled books, in charactery,
Hold like rich garners the full ripen'd grain;
When I behold, upon the night's starr'd face,
Huge cloudy symbols of a high romance,
And think that I may never live to trace
Their shadow, with the magic hand of chance;

And when I feel, fair creature of an hour,
That I shall never look upon thee more,
Never have relish in the faery power
Of unreflecting love;—then on the shore
Of the wide world I stand alone, and think
Till love and fame to nothingness do sink.

SONNETS VII

Sigmund Freud (1856-1939)

Conscience is the internal perception of the rejection of
a particular wish operating within us.

TOTEM AND TABOO

George Santayana (1863-1952)

Consciousness is the inner light kindled in the soul…a music,
strident or sweet, made by the friction of existence.

THE REALM OF TRUST

Sri Aurobindo (1872-1950)

All eyes that look on me are my sole eyes;
The one heart that beats within all breasts is mine.
The world's happiness flows through me like wine,
Its million sorrows are my agonies.
Yet all its acts are only waves that pass
Upon my surface; only for ever still
Unborn I set, timeless, intangible:
All things are shadows in my tranquil glass.
My vast transcendence holds the cosmic whirl;
I am hid in it as in the sea a pearl.

SONNETS OF COSMIC CONSCIOUSNESS

I have thrown from me the whirling dance of mind
And stand now in the spirit's silence free;
Timeless and deathless beyond creature-kind,
The center of my own eternity.
My mind is hushed in a wide and endless light,
My heart a solitude of delight and peace,
My sense ensnared by touch and sound and sight,

My body a point in white infinities.
I am the one Being's sole immobile Bliss:
No one I am, I who am all that is.
SONNETS OF COSMIC CONSCIOUSNESS

Yogaswami (1872-1964)

Why do you want to open the outside door when there is an inside door? Everything is within.
POSITIVE THOUGHTS FOR DAILY MEDITATION

G. K. Chesterton (1874-1936)

Suppose somebody in a story says "Pluck this flower and a princess will die in a castle beyond the sea," we do not know why something stirs in the subconscious, or why what is impossible seems also inevitable…. We do not know why the imagination has accepted that image before the reason can reject it; or why such correspondences seem really to correspond to something in the soul. Very deep things in our nature, some dim sense of the dependence of great things upon small, some dark suggestion that the things nearest to us stretch far beyond our power, some sacramental feeling of the magic in material substances, and many more emotions past finding out, are in an idea like that of the external soul.

THE EVERLASTING MAN

The truth is that the thing most present to the mind of man is not the economic machinery necessary to his existence, but rather that existence itself; the world which he sees when he wakes every morning and the nature of his general position in it. There is something that is nearer to him than livelihood and that is life. For once that he remembers exactly what work produces his wages and exactly what wages produce his meals, he reflects ten times that it is a fine day or it is a queer world, or wonders whether life is worth living, or wonders whether marriage is a failure, or is pleased and puzzled with his own children, or remembers his own youth, or in any such fashion vaguely reviews the mysterious lot of man. This is true of the majority even of the wage-slaves of our morbid modern industrialism, which by its hideousness and inhumanity has really forced the economic issue to the front.

THE EVERLASTING MAN

G. I. Gurdjieff (1877-1949)

In speaking of evolution it is necessary to understand from the outset that no mechanical evolution is possible. The evolution of man is the evolution of consciousness and "consciousness" cannot evolve unconsciously. The evolution of man is the evolution of his will and "will" cannot evolve involuntarily. The evolution of man is the evolution of his power of doing, and "doing" cannot be the result of things which "happen."

LETTER TO OUSPENSKY

The Mother (1878-1973)

The ordinary consciousness lives in a constant state of fidgeting, it's frightening when you realize it! As long as you are not aware of it, it's perfectly natural, but when you become aware of it, you wonder how people don't go crazy, it's a grace! It is a kind of microscopic trepidation. Oh, how horrible!

And its the same for everything: for world events and natural cataclysms and mankind, for earthquakes and tidal waves,

for volcanic eruptions, floods and wars, for revolutions
and people who take their own lives without even knowing
why— everywhere, they are all impelled by something; behind
that "fidgeting," there's a will for disorder seeking to prevent
the establishment of harmony. It's in each individual in each
group and in Nature.

SATPREM, *THE MIND OF THE CELLS*

Pierre Teilhard de Chardin (1881-1955)

My education and my religion had always led me obediently
to accept—without much reflection, it is true—a fundamental
heterogeneity between Matter and Spirit, between Body and
Soul, between Unconscious and Conscious. These were to
me two "substances" that differed in nature,…and it was
important, I was told, to maintain at all cost that the first of
these two (my divine Matter!) was no more than the humble
servant of the second, if not, indeed, its enemy. Thus the
second of the two (Spirit) was by that very fact henceforth
reduced for me to being no more than a Shadow. In principle,

it is true, I was compelled to venerate this shadow but, emotionally and intellectually speaking, I did not in fact have any live interest in it. You can well imagine, accordingly, how strong was my inner feeling of release and expansion when I took my first still hesitant steps into an 'evolutive' Universe, and saw that the dualism in which I had hitherto been enclosed was disappearing like the mist before the rising sun. Matter and Spirit: These were no longer two things but two *states* or two aspects of one and the same cosmic Stuff.

THE HEART OF THE MATTER

From the critical moment when I rejected many of the old molds in which my family life and my religion had formed me and began to wake up and express myself in terms that were really my own, I have experienced no form of self-development without some feminine eye turned on me, some feminine influence at work.

THE HEART OF THE MATTER

D. H. Lawrence (1885-1930)

He had made a passionate study of education, only to come, gradually, to the knowledge that education is nothing but the process of building up, gradually, a complete unit of consciousness. And each unit of consciousness is the living unit of that great social, religious, philosophic idea toward which mankind, like an organism seeking its final form, is laboriously growing.

PHOENIX II

Erwin Schrödinger (1887-1961)

It is possible that this unity of knowledge, feeling, and choice which you call *your own* should have sprung into being from nothingness at a given moment not so long ago; rather this knowledge, feeling, and choice are essentially and unchangeably and numerically *one* in all men, nay in all sensitive beings. But not in *this* sense—that *you* are a part, a piece, of an eternal, infinite being, an aspect or modification of it, as in Spinoza's pantheism. For *we* should have the same baffling question: Which part, which aspect are you?

What objectively differentiates it from the others? No, but inconceivably as it seems to ordinary reason, you—and all other conscious beings as such—are all in all. Hence this life of yours which you are living is not merely a piece of the entire existence, but is in a certain sense the whole; only this whole is not so constituted that it can be surveyed in one single glance.

MY VIEW OF THE WORLD

Ludwig Wittgenstein (1889-1951)
The aspects of things that are most important for us are hidden because of their simplicity and familiarity.

LECTURES ON RELIGIOUS BELIEF

Wei Wu Wei (1895-1986)
All I am is "see*ing*" when I see,
All I am is "hear*ing*" when I hear,
All I am is "sentience" when I feel,
All I am is understand*ing* when I know.

OPEN SECRET

Pure Thought is seeing thing as they appear—without arguing (thinking) about them, just "seeing, seeing, seeing," as Rumi said. Above all, without *inference*.

OPEN SECRET

We are all part of the party: The party goes on even if we fall asleep, but our falling asleep is also part of the party.

OPEN SECRET

Anandamayi Ma (1896-1982)

There is little to tell. My consciousness has never associated itself with this temporary body. Before I came on the earth, "I was the same." As a little girl, "I was the same." I grew into womanhood, but still "I was the same." When the family in which I had been born made arrangements to have this body married, "I was the same."…And in front of you now, "I am the same." Ever afterward, though the dance of creation

change around me, "I shall be the same." Now and always
one with That, "I am the same."
AUTOBIOGRAPHY OF A YOGI

E. Recejac (d. 1899)

When mystical activity is at its height, we find consciousness
possessed by a sense of a being at once *excessive and
identical* with the self: great enough to be God; interior
enough to be me.
ESSAY ON THE BASES OF THE MYSTIC KNOWLEDGE

Thomas Merton (1915-1968)

We stumble and fall constantly even when we are most
enlightened. But when we are in true spiritual darkness,
we do not even know that we have fallen.
QUOTED IN *THE SOUL: AN ARCHEOLOGY*,
CLAUDIA SETZER

Alan Watts (1915-1973)

As the fish doesn't know water, man is ignorant of space.
Consciousness is concerned only with changing and varying
details; it ignores constants—especially constant backgrounds.
Thus only very exceptional people are aware of what is basic
to everything.

CLOUD-HIDDEN, WHEREABOUTS UNKNOWN:
A MOUNTAIN JOURNAL

The spiritual is not to be separated from the material, nor
the wonderful from the ordinary. We need, above all, to
disentangle ourselves from habits of speech and thought
which set the two apart, making it impossible for us to see
that *this*—the immediate, everyday, and present experience—
is IT, the entire and ultimate point of the existence of the
universe. But the recognition that the two are one comes
to pass in an elusive, though relatively common, state of
consciousness.... I believe that if this state of consciousness
could become more universal, the pretentious nonsense
which passes for the serious business of the world would
dissolve in laughter. We should see at once that the high

ideals for which we are killing and regimenting each other are empty and abstract substitutes for the unheeded miracles that surround us—not only in the obvious wonders of nature but also in the overwhelmingly uncanny fact of mere existence.

THIS IS IT: AND OTHER ESSAYS ON ZEN AND SPIRITUAL EXPERIENCE

If…consciousness ceases to ignore itself and becomes fully self-conscious, it discovers two things: (1) that it controls itself only very slightly, and is thoroughly dependent on other things—father and mother, external nature, biological processes, God or what you will, and (2) that there is no little man inside, no "I" who owns this consciousness. And if that is so, if I do not own my consciousness, and if there is even no "me" to own it, to receive it, or to put up with it, who on earth is there to be either the victim of fate or the master of nature? "What is troubling us," said Wittgenstein, "is the tendency to believe that the mind is like a little man within."

THIS IS IT: AND OTHER ESSAYS ON ZEN AND SPIRITUAL EXPERIENCE

The words which one might be tempted to use for a silent and wide-open mind are mostly terms of abuse—thoughtless, mindless, unthinking, empty-headed, and vague. Perhaps this is some measure of an innate fear of releasing the chronic cramp of consciousness by which we grasp the facts of life and manage the world. It is only to be expected that the idea of an awareness which is something other than sharp and selective fills us with considerable disquiet. We are perfectly sure that it would mean going back to the supposedly confused sensitivity of infants and animals, that we should be unable to distinguish up from down, and that we should certainly be run over by a car the first time we went out on the street.

DOES IT MATTER?

Roberto Assagioli (1888-1974)

Truly religious music.... awakens and stimulates the spiritual "germs" which exist in every one of us, waiting to come to life. It lifts us above the level of everyday consciousness, up into those higher realms where light, love, and joy ever reign.

PSYCHOSYNTHESIS: A MANUAL OF PRINCIPLES AND TECHNIQUES

Carlos Castaneda (1925-1998)

This indeed is the mystery of awareness. Human beings reek of that mystery; we reek of darkness, of things which are inexplicable. To regard ourselves in any other terms is madness. So don't demean the mystery of man in you by feeling sorry for yourself or by trying to rationalize it. Demean the stupidity of man in you by understanding it. But don't apologize for either; both are needed.

THE FIRE WITHIN

U. G. Krishnamurti (Contemporary)

All that you do makes it impossible for what already is there to express itself.

CONVERSATIONS WITH A MAN CALLED U. G.

Marion Milner (1900-1998)

I tried to learn, not from reason but from my senses. But as soon as I began to study my perception, to look at my own experience, I found that there were different ways of perceiving and that the different ways provided me with different facts. There was a narrow focus which meant seeing life as if from blinkers and with the center of awareness in my head; and there was a wide focus which meant knowing with the whole of my body, a way of looking which quite altered my perception of whatever I saw. And I found that the narrow focus way was the way of reason. If one was in the habit of arguing about life it was very difficult not to approach sensation with the same concentrated attention and so shut out its width and depth and height. But it was the wide focus way that made me happy.

A LIFE OF ONE'S OWN

Those flickering leaf-shadows playing over the heap of cut grass… The shadows are blue or green, I don't know which, but I feel them in my bones. Down into the shadows of the gully, across it through glistening space, space that hangs suspended filling the gully, so that sounds wander there, lose themselves and are drowned; beyond, there's a splash of sunlight leaping out against the darkness of forest, the gold in it flows richly in my eyes, flows through my brain in still pools of light. That pine, my eye is led up and down the straightness of its trunk, my muscles feel its roots spreading wide to hold it so upright against the hill. The air is full of sounds, sighs of wind in the trees, sighs which fade back into the overhanging silence. A bee passes, a golden ripple in the quiet air.

A LIFE OF ONE'S OWN

Sogyal Rinpoche (Contemporary)

Compassion is a far greater and nobler thing than pity. Pity has its roots in fear, and a sense of arrogance and condescension, sometimes even a smug feeling of "I'm glad it's not me."... To train in compassion, then, is to know all beings are the same and suffer in similar ways, to honor all those who suffer, and to know you are neither separate from nor superior to anyone.

THE TIBETAN BOOK OF LIVING AND DYING

Yatri (Contemporary)

When the Void looks into the mirror
It sees us.
When we look into the Void we see the mirror.
When we look in the mirror
We see the Void.
When the mirror looks into the mirror…
It laughs.

UNKNOWN MAN

CREATION

Indian Creation Myth

(Date of origin unknown, first known record 300–500)

The world is created, destroyed, and re-created in an eternally repetitive series of cycles. It continuously moves from one Maha Yuga (Great Age) to the next, with each lasting for 4,320,000 years. Each Maha Yuga consists of a series of four shorter yugas, or ages, each of which is morally worse and of shorter duration than the age that preceded it…. At the end of 1,000 Maha Yugas (Great Ages), which is one day of the life of the world, the great god Vishnu will adopt the form of Shiva-Rudra and will destroy all life on earth. He will usher in one night in the life of the world, a period lasting as long as the day…. At the end of the long night of 1,000 Maha Yugas, Vishnu will awaken. A marvelous lotus flower will emerge from his navel, and Vishnu will emerge from the lotus flower in his creative form of Brahma, creator of life on earth. The lotus will become the foundation of the three worlds.... First Brahma the creator will bring forth water, fire, air, wind, sky, and earth, with mountains and trees upon the earth. Then he will create the forms of time, as a way of organizing the universe.

Soon thereafter, Brahma will concentrate upon creating gods, demons, and human beings. First he will bring forth the demons from his buttocks. He will then cast off his body, creating the darkness we call night, which belongs to the enemies of the gods. Taking a second body, Brahma will bring forth the gods from his face. He will cast off this body as well, creating the lightness we call day, which belongs to the gods. From successive bodies, Brahma's powers of concentration will bring forth human beings and Rakshasas, snakes and birds. Then Brahma will bring forth goats, buffalo, camels, donkeys, elephants, and other animals from his arms and legs, horses from his feet, and plant life from the hair on his body.

WORLD MYTHOLOGY, DONNA ROSENBERG

Japanese Creation Myth

(Date of origin unknown, first known record 712)

In the beginning, heaven and earth were one unformed mass, similar to a shapeless egg. The lighter, clearer part remained above and, in time, became heaven. More slowly, the heavier, denser part sank below and became earth. At first, pieces of land floated about in the void as a fish floats on the surface of the sea. A detached object, shaped like a reed-shoot when it first emerges from the mud, floated in the void between heaven and earth as a cloud floats over the sea. This became the first god.

WORLD MYTHOLOGY, DONNA ROSENBERG

Mayan Creation Myth

(Date of origin unknown, first known record 1553–1558)

In the beginning, only the sky above and the sea below existed in the eternal darkness, and they were calm and silent, for nothing existed that could move or make noise. The surface of the earth had yet to rise forth from the waters. Grass and trees, stones, caves and ravines, birds and fish, crabs, animals, and human beings had yet to be created. Nothing could roar or rumble; nothing could sing or squeak; nothing could run or shake, for there was nothing but the vacant sky above and the tranquil sea below.

Hidden in the water under green and blue feathers were the Creators. These great thinkers talked quietly together in the water, alone in the universe, alone in the darkness of the eternal night. Together they decided what would be. Together they decided when the earth would rise from the waters, when the first human beings and all other forms of life would be born, what these living things would eat in order to survive, and when dawn would first flood the world with pale light…. And so they created it.

WORLD MYTHOLOGY, DONNA ROSENBERG

The Rig Veda (c. 1200-900 BCE)

There then was neither Aught nor Nought,
No air nor sky beyond.
What covered all? Where rested all?
In watery gulf profound?

Nor death was there, nor deathlessness,
Nor change of night and day.
That One breathed calmly, self-sustained:
Nor else beyond It lay.
Gloom hid in gloom existed first—
One sea eluding view.
That One, a void in chaos wrapt,
By inward fervor grew.
Within It first arose desire,
The primal germ of mind,
Which nothing with existence links,
As sages searching find.
The kindling ray that shot across
The dark and drear abyss,
Was it beneath? Or high aloft?
What bard can answer this?
There fecundating powers were found,
and mighty forces strove,
A self-supporting mass beneath,
And energy above.

Who knows, whoe'er hath told, from whence
This vast creation rose?
No gods had then been born, who then can
e'er the truth disclose?
Whence sprang this world, and whether framed
By hand divine or no,
Its lord in heaven alone can tell,
If even he can show.

HYMN 129

The Upanishads (c. 900-600 BCE)

Just as a spider voids its body by a thread, just as tiny sparks
go forth from a fire, even so from this Self all the organs, all
the worlds, all the gods, all things go forth.

BRHAD UPANISHAD

As its web a spider emits and draws in, just as plants arise on
the earth and wither, just as hair develops on living persons,
even so this world from the Self arises.

MUNDAKA UPANISHAD

Lao Tzu (c. 6th Century BCE)

One who has a man's wings
And a woman's also
Is in himself a womb of the world:
And, being a womb of the world,
Continuously, endlessly,
Gives birth;
One who, preferring light,
Prefers darkness also
Is in himself an image of the world
And, being an image of the world,
Is continuously, endlessly
The dwelling of creation.

TAO TE CHING

Chuang Tzu (369-286 BCE)

If there was a beginning, then there was a time before that beginning, and a time before the time which was before the time of that beginning. If there is existence, there must have been nonexistence. And if there was a time when nothing existed, then there must have been a time when even nothing did not exist. All of a sudden, nothing came into existence. Could one then really say whether it belongs to the category of existence or of nonexistence? Even the very words I have just now uttered, I cannot say whether they say something or not.

ON LEVELING ALL THINGS

Huai-Nan Tzu (1st Century BCE)

Before heaven and earth had taken vague form all was vague and amorphous. Therefore it was called The Great Beginning. The Great Beginning produced emptiness and emptiness produced the universe…. The combined essences of heaven and earth became the yin and yang, the concentrated essences of the yin and yang became the four seasons, and the scattered essences of the four seasons became the myriad creatures of the world.

SOURCES OF CHINESE TRADITION

Virgil (70-19 BCE)

With Jove I begin.

ECLOGUES

Solomon ben Judah Ibn Gabirol (c. 1021-1058)

It is impossible to describe the Will. One may only approximate its definition by saying that it is a divine Power, creating matter and form and holding them together, and that it is diffused from the highest to the lowest…. It is this Power which moves and directs everything.

FOUNTAIN OF LIFE

Hakim Sanai (12th Century)

Your intellect is just a hotch-potch
of guesswork and thought,
limping over the face of the earth;
wherever they are, he [God] is not;
they are contained within his creation.

Man and his reason are just the latest
ripening plants in his garden.
Whatever you assert about his nature,
you are bound to be out of your depth,
like a blind man trying to describe
the appearance of his own mother.
While reason is still tracking down the secret,
you end your quest on the open field of love.

THE WALLED GARDEN OF TRUTH

Gustave Flaubert (1821-1880)

The artist must be in his work as God is in creation, invisible
and all-powerful; his presence should be felt everywhere, but
he should never be seen.

MADAME BOVARY

Paul Valéry (1871-1945)

God made everything out of nothing. But the nothingness
shows through.

MAUVAISES PENSÉES ET AUTRES

G. K. Chesterton (1874-1936)

In a hundred forms we are told that heaven and earth were once lovers, or were once at one, when some upstart thing, often some undutiful child, thrust them apart; and the world was built on an abyss; upon a division and a parting…. One of its most charming versions was that…a little pepper-plant grew taller and taller and lifted the whole sky like a lid….

THE EVERLASTING MAN

The Australian aborigines…have a story about a giant frog who had swallowed the sea and all the waters of the world; and who was only forced to spill them by being made to laugh. All the animals with all their antics passed before him and, like Queen Victoria, he was not amused. He collapsed at last before an eel who stood delicately balanced on the tip of its tail, doubtless with a rather desperate dignity. Any amount of fine fantastic literature might be made out of that fable. There is philosophy in that laughter.

THE EVERLASTING MAN

Sri Ramana Maharshi (1879-1950)

There is neither creation nor destruction,
Neither destiny nor free will,
Neither path nor achievement;
This is the final truth.

COLLECTED WORKS

Hazrat Inayat Khan (1882-1927)

Music is the basis of the whole creation. In reality the whole of creation is music, and what we call music is simply a miniature of the original music, which is creation itself, expressed in tone and rhythm.

THE SUFI MESSAGE OF HAZRAT INAYAT KHAN:
THE ART OF PERSONALITY

D. H. Lawrence (1885-1930)

Cosmology, however, considers only the creation of the material universe, and according to the scientific idea life itself is but a product of reactions in the material universe. This is palpably wrong.

THE TWO PRINCIPLES

Nikos Kazantzakis (1885-1957)

This, I thought, is how great visionaries and poets see everything—as if for the first time. Each morning they see a new world before their eyes; they do not really see it, they create it.

ZORBA THE GREEK

Robert Graves (1895-1985)

In the beginning, Eurynome, the Goddess of All Things, rose naked from Chaos, but found nothing substantial for her feet to rest upon, and therefore divided the sea from the sky, dancing lonely upon its waves. She danced towards the south, and the wind set in motion behind her seemed something new and apart with which to begin a work of creation. Wheeling about, she caught hold of this north wind, rubbed it between her hands, and behold! the great serpent Ophion. Eurynome danced to warm herself, wildly and more wildly, until Ophion, grown lustful, coiled about those divine limbs and was moved to couple with her…. Next, she assumed the form of a dove, brooding on the waves and, in due process of time, laid the Universal Egg. At her bidding, Ophion coiled

seven times about this egg, until it hatched and split in two.
Out tumbled all things that exist, her children: sun, moon,
planets, stars, the earth with its mountains and rivers, its
trees, herbs, and living creatures.

PELASGIAN CREATION MYTH, *THE GREEK MYTHS*

Sarvepalli Radhakrishnan (1888-1975)

The world process with its order and creativity requires for its
explanation a creative power. For however far we may travel
backward in space or time, we cannot jump out of space or
time, and we cannot account for space-time structure. The
rationality of the universe suggests that the creative power is
mind or spirit. There is no reason why we should identify it
with vital force or life, as Bergson suggests, and not with spirit,
for spirit is the highest we know…. The Indian figure of lila
makes the creation of the universe an act of playfulness. Play
is generally the expression of ideal possibilities. It is its own
end and its own continuous reward…. Though the creation
of the world is an incident in the never-ending activity of the
Absolute, it satisfies a deep want in God.

AN IDEALIST VIEW OF LIFE

Osho (1931-1990)

There has been no creation. How can there be "the beginning"? The creation is continuous; it is creativity. Back you move, you will not find the beginning, ahead you go, you will not find the end. It is beginningless, endless creative energy. So in the first place there was no beginning. God never created the world—there is no God.

DISCOURSES

Paul Davies (Contemporary)

These days most cosmologists and astronomers back the theory that there was indeed a creation, about eighteen billion years ago, when the physical universe burst into existence in an awesome explosion popularly know as the 'big bang.'

GOD AND THE NEW PHYSICS

John A. O'Brien (Contemporary)

As the tiny mountain rivulet as well as the majestic lake and river, after many windings and turnings, all trace their course at last down to the ocean's mighty shore, so all things and all living creatures, all trace their origin and existence back to God, their Creator.

THE ORIGIN OF MAN

DEATH

The Epic of Gilgamesh (3rd Millennium BCE)

There is no permanence. Do we build a house to stand forever, do we seal a contract to hold for all time? Do brothers divide an inheritance to keep forever, does the flood-time of rivers endure?… From the days of old there is no permanence. The sleeping and the dead, how alike they are, they are like a painted death. What is there between the master and the servant when both have fulfilled their doom? When the Anunnaki, the judges [of the dead], come together, and Mammetun the mother of destinies, together they decree the fates of men. Life and death they allot but the day of death they do not disclose.

The Bhagavad Gita (c. 500 BCE)

He who, at the time of death, thinking of Me alone, goes forth, leaving the body, he attains unto my Being.

The Dhammapada (3rd Century BCE)

All beings tremble before danger, all fear death. When a man considers this, he does not kill or cause to kill.

THE PATH OF PERFECTION

When a man considers this world as a bubble of froth, and as the illusion of an appearance, then the king of death has no power of him.

THE PATH OF PERFECTION

One who knows the Self puts death to death.

THE PATH OF PERFECTION

The body dies, but the spirit is not entombed.

QUOTED IN *THE SOUL, AN ARCHEOLOGY*,
CLAUDIA SETZER

Sappho (c. 610–570 BCE)

Death is an evil; the gods have so judged; had it been good,
they would die.

FRAGMENT

Mahabharata, XII (4th–5th Century BCE)

Possessed by delusion, a man toils for his wife and child; but
whether he fulfills his purpose or not, he must surrender the
enjoyment thereof. When one is blessed with children and
flocks and his heart is clinging to them, Death carries him
away as doth a tiger a sleeping deer.

Socrates (469–399 BCE)

You too, gentlemen of the jury, must look forward to death
with confidence, and fix your minds on this one belief, which
is certain: that nothing can harm a good man either in life or

after death, and his fortunes are not a matter of indifference to the gods. This present experience of mine has not come about accidentally; I am quite clear that the time had come when it was better for me to die and be released from my distractions. That is why my sign (his guiding spirit) never turned me back.

PLATO'S *APOLOGY*

Epicurus (341-270 BCE)

Death is nothing to us, since when we are, death has not come, and when death has come, we are not.

FROM *DIOGENES LAËRTIUS*, BOOK 10, SEC. 125

Lucretius (c. 99-55 BCE)

Why shed tears that thou must die? For if thy past life has been one of enjoyment, and if all thy pleasures have not passed through thy mind, as through a sieve, and vanished, leaving not a rack behind, why then dost thou not, like a thankful guest, rise cheerfully from life's feast, and with a quiet mind go take thy rest.

DE RERUM NATURA

Virgil (70-19 BCE)

Naked in death upon an unknown shore.

AENEID

Seneca (c. 4 BCE-65 CE)

That day, which you fear as being the end of all things, is the birthday of your eternity.

LETTERS TO LUCILIUS

Marcus Aurelius (121-180)

The act of dying is also one of the acts of life.

MEDITATIONS

And as for death, if there be any gods, it is no grievous thing to leave the society of men. The gods will do thee no hurt, thou mayest be sure. But if it be so that there be no gods, or that they take no care of the world, why should I desire to live in a world void of gods, and of all divine providence?

MEDITATIONS

Otomo No Tabito (665-731)

Because it is the case that

Every living man

In the end dies,

While we are in the world

Let us be merry!

JAPANESE POETRY: THE UTA, ARTHUR WALEY

Wang Wei (699-761)

White hairs will never be transformed

That elixir is beyond creation

To eliminate decrepitude

Study the absolute.

"SITTING ALONE ON AN AUTUMN NIGHT,"
IN *THE POEMS OF WANG WEI*

Husayn ibn Mansur al-Hallaj (858-922)

My life is in my death, and my death is in my life.

DIWAN

Lady Sarashina (c. 1008)

That smoke we watched above her pyre
Has vanished utterly.
How can she have hoped to find the grave
Among the bamboo grasses of the plain?

AS I CROSSED A BRIDGE OF DREAMS

Milarepa (1040-1123)

Death is like a shadow cast by the sun;
I have never seen it prevented.

THE MESSAGE OF MILAREPA

Al-Ghazali (b. 1058)

The meaning of death is not the annihilation of the spirit,
but its separation from the body, and that the resurrection
and day of assembly do not mean a return to a new existence
after annihilation, but the bestowal of a new form or frame
to the spirit.

THE REVIVAL OF RELIGIOUS SCIENCES

François Rabelais (c. 1494-1553)

Je vais querir un grand peut-être…. Tirez le rideau, la farce est jouée.

(I am going to seek a great perhaps…. Pull down the curtain, the farce is ended.)

BY TRADITION, HIS LAST WORDS

Michel de Montaigne (1533-1592)

If you do not know how to die, never mind. Nature will give you full and adequate instruction on the spot. She will do this job for you neatly; do not worry yourself with the thought.

ESSAYS

If we have known how to live steadfastly and calmly, we shall know how to die in the same way. They may boast as much as they please, that "a philosopher's whole life is a contemplation of death." It seems to me, however, that it is indeed the end but not the aim of life; it is its conclusion, its extreme point, yet not its object. Life should contain its own aim, its own purposes.

ESSAYS

Sir Francis Bacon (1561-1626)

The world's a bubble, and the life of man less than a span.

THE WORLD

Who then to frail mortality shall trust
But limns on water, or but writes in dust.

THE WORLD

It is as natural to die as to be born; and to a little infant,
perhaps the one is as painful as the other.

ESSAYS

William Shakespeare (1564-1616)

Fear no more the heat of the sun
Nor the furious winter's rages;
Thou thy worldly task hast done,
Home art gone and ta'en thy wages.
Golden lads and girls all must,
As chimney-sweepers, come to dust.

CYMBELINE, IV, 2, 258

All that live must die, Passing through nature to eternity.

HAMLET, I, 2

John Donne (1572-1631)

Death be not proud, though some have called thee
Mighty and dreadful, for, thou art not so,
For, those, whom thou think'st thou dost overthrow,
Die not, poor death, nor yet can'st thou kill me.

DEATH BE NOT PROUD

Robert Burton (1557-1640)

The fear of death is worse than death.

ANATOMY OF MELANCHOLY

Tales from the Thousand and One Nights (18th Century)

[The King] reigned through many joyful years, until he was
visited by the Destroyer of all earthly pleasures, the Leveller
of mighty kings and humble peasants.

THE TALE OF MA'ARUF, THE COBBLER

Henry Fielding (1707-1754)

It hath often been said that it is not death but dying that is terrible.

AMELIA

Samuel Johnson (1709-1784)

Depend upon it, Sir, when a man knows he is to be hanged in a fortnight, it concentrates his mind wonderfully.

QUOTED IN *LIFE OF JOHNSON*, JAMES BOSWELL

Chief Seattle (1786-1866)

There is no death. Only a change of worlds.

QUOTED IN *THE SPIRITUAL LEGACY OF THE AMERICAN INDIAN*, JOSEPH EPES BROWN

Percy Bysshe Shelley (1792-1822)

Life, like a dome of many-colored glass,
Stains the white radiance of Eternity.
Until death tramples it to fragments.

ADONAIS

Henry Wadsworth Longfellow (1807-1882)

The grave is but a covered bridge leading from light to light, through a brief darkness.

A COVERED BRIDGE AT LUCERNE

Emily Dickinson (1830-1886)

Because I could not stop for Death
He kindly stopped for me
The Carriage held but just Ourselves
And Immortality.

POEM NO. 712

Phillips Brooks (1835-1893)

Death is the enlightener. The essential thing concerning it must be that it opens the closed eyes, draws down the veil of blinding mortality, and lets the man see spiritual things.

PERENNIALS

John Muir (1838-1914)

Let children walk with Nature, let them see the beautiful blendings and communions of death and life, their joyous, inseparable unity, as taught in woods and meadows…and they will learn that death is stingless indeed, and as beautiful as life.

A THOUSAND-MILE WALK TO THE GULF

Henry van Dyke (1852-1933)

Some people are so afraid to die that they never begin to live.

LETTERS

Cecil Rhodes (1853-1902)

So little done, so much to do.

LAST WORDS

Dora Carrington (1872-1941)

If this is death, I don't think much of it.

LAST WORDS

W. Somerset Maugham (1874-1965)

Dying is a very dull, dreary affair. And my advice to you is to have nothing whatever to do with it.

A WRITER'S NOTEBOOK

Thomas Mann (1875-1955)

The only religious way to think of death is as part and parcel of life.

THE MAGIC MOUNTAIN

Elizabeth Arden (1878-1966)

Death not merely ends life, it also bestows upon it a silent completeness, snatched from the hazardous flux to which all things human are subject.

THE LIFE OF THE MIND

Nikos Kazantzakis (1885-1957)

Luckless man has raised what he thinks is an impassable barrier round his poor little existence. He takes refuge there and tries to bring a little order and security into his life. A little happiness. Everything must follow the beaten track, the sacrosanct routine, and comply with safe and simple rules. Inside this enclosure, fortified against the fierce attacks of the unknown, his petty certainties, crawling about like centipedes, go unchallenged. There is only one formidable enemy, mortally feared and hated: the Great Certainty [death].

ZORBA THE GREEK

Dorothy Parker (1893-1967)

It costs me never a stab nor squirm
To tread by chance upon a worm.
"Aha, my little dear," I say,
"Your clan will pay me back one day."

THOUGHTS FOR A SUNSHINY MORNING

Sylvia Plath (1932-1963)

Dying is an art, like everything else.

LADY LAZARUS

Morris B. Abram (Contemporary)

A painting on a canvas of infinite size, worked on eternally, would be without focus, meaning, and probably without beauty. A painting, as life, needs limits. While I have an almost insatiable craving for knowledge, I believe death to be the final and perhaps greatest teacher—the one that provides the key to the ultimate questions life has never answered. In my darkest hours I have been consoled by the thought that death at least is a payment for the answer of life's haunting secrets.

THE WALL STREET JOURNAL

Woody Allen (Contemporary)

It's not that I'm afraid to die. I just don't want to be there when it happens.

WITHOUT FEATHERS, "DEATH"

Carlos Castaneda (1925-1998)

An immense amount of pettiness is dropped if your death makes a gesture to you, or if you catch a glimpse of it, or if you just have the feeling that your companion is there watching you…. Death is the only wise adviser that we have. Whenever you feel…that everything is going wrong and you're about to be annihilated, turn to your death and ask if that is so. Your death will tell you that you're wrong; that nothing really matters outside its touch. Your death will tell you, "I haven't touched you yet."

JOURNEY TO IXTLAN

Elisabeth Kübler-Ross (Contemporary)

It is those who have not really lived—who have left issues unsettled, dreams unfulfilled, hopes shattered, and who have let the real things in life (loving and being loved by others, contributing in a positive way to other people's happiness and welfare, finding out what things are *really* you) pass them by—who are most reluctant to die.

IN *WEAVERS OF WISDOM*, ANNE BANCROFT

Peter Lorie (Contemporary)

If I lie down one day and die in my sleep,
How will I know if I still dream,
A dream of death in life or a dream of life in death.
That maybe I will wake again a child still dreaming.
And how will I know which life I have left before sleep,
And which life I have come to on waking?
Would I dream of dying or die of dreaming?
And is there a difference?

UNTITLED

G. S. Merriam (Contemporary)

No one who is fit to live need fear to die.... To us here, death is the most terrible word we know. But when we have tasted its reality, it will mean to us birth, deliverance, a new creation of ourselves.

A LIVING FAITH

Norman O. Brown (Contemporary)

This incapacity to die, ironically but inevitably, throws mankind out of the actuality of living, which for all normal animals is at the same time dying; the result is the denial of life (repression). The incapacity to accept death turns the death instinct into its destructively human and distinctly morbid form. The distraction of human life to the war against death, by the same inevitable irony, results in death's dominion over life.

LIFE AGAINST DEATH: THE PSYCHOANALYTIC MEANING OF HISTORY

Sogyal Rinpoche (Contemporary)

In the Buddhist approach, life and death are seen as one whole, where death is the beginning of another chapter of life. Death is a mirror in which the entire meaning of life is reflected.

THE TIBETAN BOOK OF LIVING AND DYING

Antonin Sertillages (Contemporary)

When death is spoken of as a tearing asunder, we forget that it tears especially the veil of appearances and of deceptions which conceal from our view the depth of reality and of others and ourselves.

RECOLLECTIONS

DREAM
AND ILLUSION

The Bhagavad Gita (c. 500 BCE)

Never the spirit was born; the spirit shall cease to be never;
Never was time it was not; End and Beginnings are dreams!
Birthless and deathless and changeless
Remaineth the spirit forever…

Chuang Tzu (369-286 BCE)

I do not know whether I was then a man dreaming I was
a butterfly, or whether I am now a butterfly dreaming
I am a man.

ON LEVELING ALL THINGS

Murasaki Shikibu (c. 974-1031)

A night of endless dreams, inconsequent and wild, is this my life; none more worth telling than the rest.

THE TALE OF GENJI

Atisa (982-1054)

Think that all phenomena are like dreams.

SEVEN POINTS OF MIND TRAINING

Hakim Sanai (12th Century)

All mankind is asleep,
living in a desolate world;
the desire to transcend this is mere habit and custom,
Not religion—idle fairy tales.

THE WALLED GARDEN OF TRUTH

Saigyo Hoshi (1118-1190)

Since I am convinced
That Reality is in no way
Real,
How am I to admit
That dreams are dreams?

JAPANESE POETRY: THE UTA, ARTHUR WALEY

Oscar Wilde (1854-1900)

A dreamer is one who can only find his way by moonlight,
and his punishment is that he sees the dawn before the rest
of the world.

THE CRITIC AS ARTIST

William Butler Yeats (1865-1939)

I have spread my dreams under your feet;
Tread softly, because you tread on my dreams.

HE WISHES FOR THE CLOTHES OF HEAVEN

Hermann Hesse (1877-1962)

When anyone reads anything which he wishes to study, he does not despise the letters and punctuation marks, and call them illusion, chance, and worthless shells, but he reads them, he studies them, and loves them letter by letter. But I, who wished to read the book of the world and the book of my own nature, did presume to despise the letters and signs. I called the world of appearances, illusion. I called my eyes and tongue, chance. Now it is over; I have awakened. I have indeed awakened and have only been born today.

SIDDHARTHA

Osho (1931-1990)

I don't think you have two hours in a day without dreams, because if you have two hours without dreams, fully awake, those two hours will become your meditation. They will reveal immensely valuable secrets to you.

DISCOURSES

Carlos Castaneda (1925-1998)

"And what is real?" don Juan asked me very calmly.

"This, what we're looking at, is real," I said, pointing to the surroundings.

"But so was the bridge you saw last night, and so was the forest and everything else."

"But if they are real, where are they now?"

"They are right here. If you had enough power you could call them back. Right now, you cannot do that because you think it is very helpful to keep on doubting and nagging. It isn't, my friend, it isn't. There are worlds upon worlds, right here in front of us."

THE POWER OF DREAMING

Robert Lawlor (Contemporary)

The higher the initiation, the more an individual lives in the awareness of this Dreamtime reality and the stronger the ancestral soul will be at the time of death.

VOICES OF THE FIRST DAY

Llewelyn Powys (1884-1939)

It is the stupidity of our minds that prevents us from seeing existence as a mystery wilder that the dreams of Devil or God.

EARTH MEMORIES

Keith Thompson (Contemporary)

That way you would whimper and tremble during dreams. The deep breezy soul-breath that came each time we reached for you. Your animal warmth joining ours.

QUOTED IN *THE SOUL: AN ARCHEOLOGY*,
CLAUDIA SETZER

EMOTION

The Upanishads (c. 900-600 BCE)

A man whose mind wanders among desires, and is longing for objects of desires, goes again to life and death according to his desires. But he who possesses the End of all longing, and whose self has found fulfilment, even in this life his desires will fade away.

MUNDAKA UPANISHAD

Sappho (c. 610-570 BCE)

When anger spreads through the breast, guard thy tongue from barking idly.

FRAGMENT

Aristotle (384-322 BCE)

It is the nature of desire not to be satisfied, and most men live only for the gratification of it. The beginning of reform is not so much to equalize property as to train the noble sort of natures not to desire more, and to prevent the lower from getting more.

POLITICS

Old Testament

He who is slow to anger is better than the mighty, and he who rules his spirit than he who takes a city.

PROVERBS 16:32

Shantideva (8th Century)

If things were brought into being by choice,
Then since no one wishes to suffer,
Suffering would not occur.

A GUIDE TO THE BODHISATTVA'S WAY OF LIFE

Milarepa (1040-1123)

All worldly pursuits have but one unavoidable and inevitable end, which is sorrow; acquisitions end in dispersion; buildings in destruction; meetings in separation; births in death. Knowing this, one should, from the very first, renounce acquisitions and storing-up, and building, and meeting; and, faithful to the commands of an eminent Guru, set about realizing the Truth. That alone is the best of religious observances.

THE MESSAGE OF MILAREPA

Kabir (c. 1440-1518)

The lock of error shuts the gate, open it with the key of love:
Thus, by opening the door thou shalt wake the Beloved.
Kabir says: "O brother! Do not pass by such good fortune
as this."

ONE HUNDRED POEMS OF KABIR

Saint John of the Cross (1542-1591)

To reach satisfaction in all, desire its possession in nothing.
To come to possess all, desire the possession of nothing.
To arrive at being all, desire to be nothing. To come to the
knowledge of all, desire the knowledge of nothing.

THE ASCENT OF MOUNT CARMEL

Edith Cavell (1865-1915)

Standing, as I do, in the view of God and eternity I realize that
patriotism is not enough. I must have no hatred or bitterness
towards anyone.

LAST WORDS AS REPORTED IN THE *TIMES* NEWSPAPER
(LONDON)

Mohandas K. Gandhi (1869-1948)

I have learnt through bitter experience the one supreme
lesson to conserve my anger, and as heat conserved is
transmuted into energy, even so our anger controlled can be
transmuted into a power which can move the world.

QUOTED IN *THE SOUL: AN ARCHAEOLOGY*,
CLAUDIA SETZER

H. L. Mencken (1880-1956)

Fear of death and fear of life both become piety.

MINORITY REPORT

Nikos Kazantzakis (1885-1957)

Once when I was a kid—this'll show you—I was mad on cherries. I had no money, so I couldn't buy many at a time, and when I'd eaten all I could buy I still wanted more. Day and night I thought of nothing but cherries. I foamed at the mouth; it was torture! But one day I got mad, or ashamed, I don't know which. Anyway, I just felt cherries were doing what they liked with me and it was ludicrous. So what did I do? I got up one night, searched my father's pockets and found a silver mejidie and pinched it. I was up early the next morning, went to the market-gardener, and bought a basket o' cherries. I settled down in a ditch and began eating. I stuffed and stuffed till I was all swollen out. My stomach began to ache and I was sick. Yes, boss, I was thoroughly sick, and from that day to this I've never wanted a cherry. I couldn't bear the sight of them. I was saved. I could say to any cherry: I don't need you any more. And I did the same thing later with wine and tobacco. I still drink and smoke, but at any second, if I want to, whoop! I can cut it out. I'm not ruled by passion.

ZORBA THE GREEK

D. H. Lawrence (1885-1930)

A man cannot create desire in himself, nor cease at will from desiring. Desire, in any shape or form, is primal, whereas the will is secondary, derived. The will can destroy, but it cannot create.

PHOENIX II

C. S. Lewis (1898-1963)

If I find I have a desire which no experience in this world can satisfy, the most probable explanation is that I was made for another world.

QUOTED IN *THE SOUL: AN ARCHAEOLOGY*, CLAUDIA SETZER

Albert Camus (1913-1960)

Like great works, deep feelings always mean more than they
are conscious of saying. The regularity of an impulse or a
repulsion in a soul is encountered again in habits of doing or
thinking, is reproduced in consequences of which the soul
itself knows nothing. Great feelings take with them their own
universe, splendid or abject. They light up with their passion
an exclusive world in which they recognize their climate.
There is a universe of jealousy, or ambition, of selfishness
or of generosity. A universe—in other words a metaphysic
and an attitude of mind. What is true of already specialized
feelings will be even more so of emotions basically as
indeterminate, simultaneously as vague and as "definite,"
as remote and as "present" as those furnished us by beauty
or aroused by absurdity.

THE MYTH OF SISYPHUS

Alan Watts (1915-1973)

It is surely obvious that how you do things depends crucially upon how you feel. If you feel inwardly isolated from the natural world, your dealings with it will tend to be hostile and aggressive. It is not so much a matter of what you do as of how you do it, not so much the content as the style of action adopted. It is easy enough to see this in leading or persuading other people, for one and the same communication may have quite opposite results according to the style or feeling with which it is given. Yet this is equally true in dealing with inanimate nature and with our own inner nature—with our instincts and appetites. They will yield to intelligence much more agreeably to the extent that we feel ourselves to be one with them, or, to put it in another way, to be in relationship to them, to have the unity of mutual interdependence.

THIS IS IT: AND OTHER ESSAYS ON ZEN AND SPIRITUAL EXPERIENCE

Osho (1931–1990)

Life up to now has been corrupted by ambition. There is no other poison which is more potent than ambition because it kills you and yet keeps you breathing. Ambition turns you into vegetables, and the lure of ambition is given to every child with the mother's milk. From the very first moment, his whole life is being based on principles of destructiveness. Nothing destroys more than ambitiousness.

DISCOURSES

Sidney Greenberg (1917–2003)

For all the unkind things said about envy, it would only be fair to acknowledge that not all envy is destructive. If envy leads us to work hard and to improve our skills, it becomes a stimulant to self-improvement. God has given us no quality that cannot be used for good.

SAY YES TO LIFE

Desmond Tutu (Contemporary)

A jealous person is doubly unhappy—over what he has, which is judged inferior, and over what he has not, which is judged superior. Such a person is doubly removed from knowing the true blessing of creation.

AN AFRICAN PRAYER BOOK

ENLIGHTENMENT

The Upanishads (c. 900-600 BCE)

Then Usata Akrayana asked him: "O Yajnavalka!" he said.
   "Explain to me what is the Brahman, immediate and
   direct, which is the Self within all."
"It is your Self within all."
"O Yajnavalka! Which of the Selves is it that is within all?"
"It is your Self within all which breathes in by your
   breathing in."
…You cannot see the Seer of seeing;
 you cannot hear the Hearer of hearing;
 you cannot think the Thinker of thinking;
 you cannot know the Knower of knowing.
 That is your Self within all.

BRHAD UPANISHAD

Lao Tzu (c. 6th Century BCE)

He who knows others is wise;
He who knows himself is enlightened.

TAO TE CHING

Whosoever stands on tiptoe does not stand firmly. Whosoever
stands with legs astride will not advance. Whosoever wants
to shine will not be enlightened. Whosoever wants to be
someone will not become resplendent. Whosoever glorifies
himself does not accomplish works. Whosoever boasts
of himself will not be exalted. For Tao he is like kitchen
refuse and a festering sore. And all the creatures loathe him.
Therefore: Whosoever has Tao does not linger with these.

TAO TE CHING

Going back to the origin is called peace; it means reversion to
destiny. Reversion to destiny is called eternity. He who knows
eternity is called enlightened.

TAO TE CHING

The Bhagavad Gita (c. 500 BCE)

In this world, aspirants may find enlightenment by two different paths. For the contemplative is the path of knowledge; for the active is the path of selfless action.

Heraclitus (c. 4th Century BCE)

Everything flows, nothing stays still.

CRATYLUS

Chuang Tzu (369-286 BCE)

To have been cast in this human form is to us already a source of joy. How much greater joy beyond our conception to know that that which is now in human form may undergo countless transitions, with only the infinite to look forward to? Therefore it is that the Sage rejoices in that which can never be lost, but endures always. For if we emulate those who can accept graciously long age or short life and the vicissitudes of events, how much more that which informs all creation on which all changing phenomena depend?

THE GREAT SUPREME

For all men strive to grasp what they do not know, while none strive to grasp what they already know; and all strive to discredit what they do not excel in, while none strive to discredit what they do excel in. This is why there is chaos.

OPENING TRUNKS

The First Book of Enoch
(3rd Century BCE—3rd Century CE)

Hear, child, from the time when the Lord anointed me with the ointment of his glory, there has been no food in me and my soul remembers not earthly enjoyment, neither do I want anything earthly.

THE LOST BOOKS OF THE BIBLE AND THE FORGOTTEN BOOKS OF EDEN

Bhagwan Shree Patanjali (2nd Century BCE)

This Samadhi completes the transformation and fulfils the purpose of evolution. Now the process by which evolution unfolds through time is understood. This is Enlightenment.

YOGA SUTRAS

Sosan (Seng-t'san)
The Third Zen Patriarch (c. 600)

One in All,

All in One—

If only this is realized,

No more worry about your not being perfect.

ON BELIEVING IN MIND

Anne Boleyn (1507-1536)

What will be, will be, grumble who may.

MOTTO EMBROIDERED ON SERVANTS' LIVERY

Matsuo Basho (1644-1694)

Do not seek to follow in the footsteps of the men of old; seek what they sought.

THE NARROW ROAD TO THE DEEP NORTH

William Blake (1757-1827)

To see a world in a grain of sand
And a heaven in a wild flower,
Hold infinity in the palm of your hand
And eternity in an hour.

AUGURIES OF INNOCENCE

Fyodor Dostoevsky (1821-1881)

Reality is infinitely various when compared to the deductions
of abstract thought, even those that are most cunning, and
it will not tolerate rigid, hard-and-fast distinctions. Reality
strives for diversification.

THE HOUSE OF THE DEAD

Thomas Henry Huxley (1825-1895)

Education is the instruction of the intellect in the laws of
Nature, under which name I include not merely things and
their forces, but men and their ways; and the fashioning of
the affections and of the will into an earnest and loving desire
to move in harmony with those laws.

ON THE NATURAL INEQUALITY OF MAN

Sri Aurobindo (1872-1950)

The soul and mind and life are powers of living and can grow, but cannot be cut out or made…. One can indeed help the being to grow…but even so, the growth must still come from within.

THE LIFE DIVINE

Yogaswami (1872-1964)

Running water will run faster if you remove an obstruction here and there. You need not do much more.

POSITIVE THOUGHTS FOR DAILY MEDITATION

D. H. Lawrence (1885-1930)

Never to be able to love spontaneously, never to be moved by a power greater than oneself, but always to be within one's own control, deliberate, having the choice, this was horrifying, more deadly than death. Yet how was one to escape? How could a man escape from being deliberate and unloving, except a greater power, an impersonal, imperative love should take hold of him? And if the greater power should not take hold of him, what could he do but continue in his deliberateness, without any fundamental spontaneity?

PHOENIX II

Jean Dubuffet (1901-1985)

Unless one says good-bye to what one loves, and unless one travels to completely new territories, one can expect merely a long wearing away of oneself and an eventual extinction.

QUOTED IN *THE NEW YORK TIMES*, OBITUARY, MAY 15, 1985

Orson Wells (1915-1985)

In Italy for thirty years under the Borgias they had warfare, terror, murder, bloodshed—they produced Michelangelo, Leonardo da Vinci, and the Renaissance. In Switzerland they had brotherly love, five hundred years of democracy and peace, and what did they produce? The cuckoo clock.

THE THIRD MAN

Osho (1931–1990)

For seven days I lived in a very hopeless and helpless state, but at the same time something was arising. There was no ground underneath; I was in an abyss, a bottomless abyss, but there was no fear because there was nothing to protect. There was no fear because there was nobody to be afraid. Those seven days were of tremendous transformation, total transformation.

And on the last day, the presence of a totally new energy, a new light and a new delight, became so intense that it was almost unbearable. It was as if I was exploding, as if I was going mad with blissfulness.

THE DISCIPLINE OF TRANSCENDENCE

The blind with a little courage gather around themselves the blind with less courage.

DISCOURSES

Paul Brunton (1898-1981)

When camphor burns no residue is left. The mind is the camphor; when it has resolved itself into the self without leaving the slightest trace, it is Realization.

QUOTED IN THE SOUL: AN ARCHEOLOGY, CLAUDIA SETZER

Norman Cousins (1915-1990)

Education tends to be diagrammatic and categorical, opening up no sluices in the human imagination on the wonder of beauty of their unique estate in the cosmos. Little wonder that it becomes so easy for our young to regard human hurt casually or to be uninspired by the magic of sensitivity.

SATURDAY REVIEW

John W. Gardner (Contemporary)

I think that all human systems require continuous renewal. They rigidify. They get stiff in the joints. They forget what they cared about. The forces against it are nostalgia and the enormous appeal of having things the way they have always been, appeals to a supposedly happy past. But we've got to move on.

THE NEW YORK TIMES, JULY 21, 1989

D. S. Sarma (Contemporary)

The ultimate aim of man is liberation; liberation not only from the bondage of the flesh, but also from the limitation of a finite being. In other words, *moksha* means becoming a perfect spirit like the Supreme Spirit.... But the law of *Karma* postulates that every individual has to pass through a series of lives either on earth or somewhere else before he attains *moksha* or liberation.

THE RELIGION OF THE HINDUS

Thich Nhat Hanh (Contemporary)

There is no enlightenment outside of daily life.

ZEN KEYS

FREEDOM

Proverb

Lean liberty is better than fat slavery.

The Bhagavad Gita (c. 500 BCE)

He whose joy is within, whose pleasure is within, and whose light is within, that devotee, being well established in the Supreme, attains to absolute freedom.

Chuang Tzu (369-286 BCE)

A thousand ounces of silver would be a great gain to me, and to be a high nobleman and minister is a most honorable position. But have you not seen the victim-ox for the ceremonial sacrifice? It is carefully fed for several years, and robed with rich embroidery that it may be fit to enter the Grand Temple. Then, when the time comes for it to do so, it would prefer to be a little

pig, but it cannot get to be so. So, go away, and do not soil me
with your presence. I would rather amuse and enjoy myself in the
midst of a filthy ditch than be subject to the rules and restrictions
in the court of a king. I have determined never to take such an
office, but prefer the enjoyment of my own free will.

OPENING TRUNKS

Hakim Sanai (12th Century)

No one knows how far it is
from nothingness to God.
As long as you cling to your self
you will wander right and left,
day and night, for thousands of years;
and when, after all that effort,
you finally open your eyes,
you will see your self, through inherent defects,
wandering round itself like the ox in a mill;
but, if, once freed from your self,
you finally get down to work,
this door will open to you within two minutes.

THE WALLED GARDEN OF TRUTH

Desiderius Erasmus (c. 1466-1536)

God commands us to pray without ceasing, to watch, to struggle, and to contend for the reward of eternal life. Why does He wish to be prayed to endlessly for that which He has already decreed to grant or not to grant, since being immutable He cannot change His decrees?

OF FREE WILL

Walt Whitman (1819-1892)

What do you suppose will satisfy the soul, except to walk free and own no superior?

LAWS FOR CREATIONS

Mikhail Naimy (1889-1988)

Happy are the staffless
They stumble not.
Happy are the homeless,
They are at home.
The stumblers only—like ourselves,

Need walk with staffs.
The home-chained only—like ourselves,
Must have a home.

THE BOOK OF MIRDAD—A LIGHTHOUSE AND A HAVEN

MIRDAD—This is the way to freedom from care and pain:

So think as if your every thought were to be etched in fire upon the sky for all and everything to see. For so, in truth it is.

So speak as if the world entire were but a single ear intent on bearing what you say. And so, in truth, it is.

So do as if your every deed were to recoil upon your heads. And so, in truth, it does.

So wish as if you were the wish. And so, in truth, you are.

So live as if your God Himself had need of you His life to live. And so, in truth, He does.

THE BOOK OF MIRDAD—A LIGHTHOUSE AND A HAVEN

True freedom is won and lost in the heart.

THE BOOK OF MIRDAD—A LIGHTHOUSE AND A HAVEN

J. Krishnamurti (1895-1986)

I have only one purpose: to make man free, to urge him toward freedom; to help him to break away from all limitations, for that alone will give him eternal happiness, will give him the unconditional realization of Self.

Because I am free, unconditioned, whole—not the part, not the relative but the whole Truth that is eternal—I desire those who seek to understand me to be free, not to follow me, not to make out of me a cage which will become a religion, a sect. Rather should they be free from all fears—from the fear of religion, from the fear of salvation, from the fear of death, from the fear of life itself. My purpose is to make man unconditionally free, for I maintain that the only spirituality is the incorruptibility of the Self which is eternal, is the harmony between reason and love.

This is the absolute, unconditioned Truth which is life itself. I want therefore to set man free, rejoicing as the bird in the clear sky, unburdened, independent, ecstatic in that freedom.

QUOTED IN PUPUL JAYAKAR, *KRISHNAMURTI—A BIOGRAPHY*

Meinhard Craighead (Contemporary)

I began to feel that freedom should beget freedom. But it didn't work. In a way, the reverse happened, and the more involved I got in my painting, which subsequently led to many outside contracts and a lot of visitors and the writing of books, the less that was liked in the community. The more I was different, the more I was rejected. And I finally had to realize that they were not interested in freedom. They were interested only in the survival of the Benedictine Order and in particular in the survival of the Abbey. So the kind of person they accepted became more and more the kind of person who would fit into the frame they allowed.

THE FEMININE MYSTIC

FRIENDSHIP

French Proverb

Hatred watches while friendship sleeps.

Confucius (551-479 BCE)

Have no friends not equal to yourself.

ANALECTS

Old Testament

Forsake not an old friend; for the new is not comparable
to him; a new friend is as new wine.

ECCLESIASTES 9:10

Hakim Sanai (12th Century)

When he [God] admits you to his presence
ask from him nothing other than himself.
When he has chosen you for a friend,
you have seen all that there is to see.
There's no duality in the world of love:
what's all this talk of 'you' and 'me'?
How can you fill a cup that's full already?

THE WALLED GARDEN OF TRUTH

Farid ud-Din Attar (c. 1120-1193)

This was no friendship, to forsake your friend,
To promise your support and at the end
Abandon him—this was sheer treachery.
Friend follows friend to hell and blasphemy—
When sorrows come a man's true friends are found;
In times of joy ten thousand gather round.

THE CONFERENCE OF THE BIRDS

Cosimo de' Medici (1389-1464)

We read that we ought to forgive our enemies; but we do not
read that we ought to forgive our friends.

LETTERS

Kabir (c. 1440-1518)

When my friend is away from me, I am depressed;
Nothing in the daylight delights me,
Sleep at night gives no rest
Who can I tell about this?
The night is dark, and long…hours go by…
because I am alone, I sit up suddenly,
fear goes through me…
Kabir says: Listen, my friend
there is one thing in the world that satisfies,
and that is a meeting with the Guest.

THE FISH IN THE SEA IS NOT THIRSTY

William Shakespeare (1564-1616)

To me, fair friend, you never can be old.

SONNET 104

Ben Jonson (c. 1573-1637)

True happiness consists not in the multitude of friends, but in the worth and choice.

VOLPONE

François La Rochefoucauld (1613-1680)

A true friend is the most precious of all possessions and the one we take the least thought about acquiring.

MAXIMS

Earl of Chesterfield (1694-1773)

There is a Spanish proverb, which says very justly, Tell me whom you live with, and I will tell you who you are.

LETTER TO HIS SON, OCTOBER 9, 1747

Samuel Johnson (1709–1784)

If a man does not make new acquaintances as he advances through life, he will soon find himself left alone.

QUOTED IN LIFE OF JOHNSON, JAMES BOSWELL

J. C. Friedrich von Schiller (1759–1805)

The zeal of friends it is that knocks me down, and not the hate of enemies.

WALLENSTEIN'S DEATH

Ralph Waldo Emerson (1803–1882)

A friend is a person with whom I may be sincere. Before him, I may think aloud.

FRIENDSHIP

A friend may well be reckoned the masterpiece of nature.

FRIENDSHIP

Mark Twain (1835-1910)

The holy passion of friendship is so sweet and steady and loyal and enduring in nature that it will last through a whole lifetime, if not asked to lend money.

"PUDD'NHEAD WILSON'S CALENDAR,"
IN PUDD'NHEAD WILSON

Henry Brooks Adams (1838-1918)

Friends are born, not made.

THE EDUCATION OF HENRY ADAMS

One friend in a life is much, two are many, three are hardly possible.

THE EDUCATION OF HENRY ADAMS

Colette (1873-1954)

My true friends have always given me that supreme proof of devotion, a spontaneous aversion for the man I loved.

BREAK OF DAY

E. M. Forster (1879–1970)

If I had to choose between betraying my country and
betraying my friend, I hope I should have the guts to betray
my country.

"WHAT I BELIEVE," IN *TWO CHEERS FOR DEMOCRACY*

E. B. White (1899–1985)

It is not often that someone comes along who is a true friend
and a good writer.

CHARLOTTE'S WEB

Dag Hammarskjöld (1905–1961)

Friendship needs no words—it is solitude delivered from the
anguish of loneliness.

MARKINGS

GOOD AND EVIL

Lao Tzu (c. 6th Century BCE)

I find good people good
And I find bad people good
If I am good enough.

TAO TE CHING

Mencius (372-289 BCE)

In good years the children of the people are most of them good, and in bad years they are most of them evil. It is not owing to their natural endowments conferred by Heaven, that they are thus different. It is owing to the circumstances in which they allow their minds to be ensnared and devoured that they appear so (as in the latter case).

BOOK VI

Juvenal (65-127)

No evil man is happy.

THE SATIRES

The Mishna (c. 200)

Rabbi Jannai said: "It is beyond our power to explain either the prosperity of the wicked or the afflictions of the righteous."

THE TALMUD QUOTED IN THE WORLD'S GREAT SCRIPTURES, LEWIS BROWNE

Saint Thomas Aquinas (1224/5-1274)

Every prudent man tolerates a lesser evil for fear of preventing a greater good.

DE VERITATE

Jami (1414-1492)

Souzani

I am a thousand times more evil
than anything you know of evil:
in this no one knows me
as I know myself.
Outwardly I am evil,
but inwardly I am even more so.
God and I, we know
my exterior and my interior.
Satan may be my guide
in the occasional venial sin;
but in a hundred deadly sins
I show Satan the way.

THE ABODE OF SPRING

Thomas Lodge (1558-1625)

Devils are not so black as they are painted.

ROSALYNDE

William Shakespeare (1564-1616)

This is the foul fiend Flibbertigibbet. He begins at curfew, and walks till the first cock. He gives the web and the pin, squints the eye, and makes the harelip; mildews the white wheat, and hurts the poor creature of earth.

KING LEAR, III, 4, 116

The Prince of Darkness is a gentleman.

KING LEAR, III, 4, 146

Blaise Pascal (1623-1662)

Men never do evil so completely and cheerfully as when they do it from religious conviction.

PENSÉES

Daniel Defoe (c. 1659-1731)

Wherever God erects a house of prayer,
The Devil always builds a chapel there,
And 'twill be found upon examination,
The latter has the largest congregation.

THE TRUE-BORN ENGLISHMAN

Edmund Burke (1729-1797)

All that is necessary for the triumph of evil is that good men do nothing.

SPEECH

John Henry Newman (1801-1890)

If Thou sendest evil upon us, it is in love. All the evils of the physical world are intended for the good of Thy creatures, or are the unavoidable attendants on that good. And Thou turnest that evil into good. Thou visitest men with evil to bring them to repentance, to increase their virtue to gain for them greater good hereafter. Nothing is done in vain, but has its gracious end. Thou dost punish, yet in wrath Thou dost remember mercy.

MEDITATIONS AND DEVOTIONS

Ellen Key (1849-1926)

All philanthropy—no age has seen more of it than our own—is only a savory fumigation burning at the mouth of a sewer. This incense offering makes the air more endurable to passersby, but it does not hinder the infection in the sewer from spreading.

THE CENTURY OF THE CHILD

Margot Asquith (1864–1945)

Riches are overestimated in the Old Testament: the good and successful man received too many animals, wives, apes, she-goats, and peacocks.

THE AUTOBIOGRAPHY OF MARGOT ASQUITH

G. K. Chesterton (1874–1936)

If I had been a Heathen,
I'd have praised the purple vine,
My slaves would dig the vineyards,
And I would drink the wine;
But Higgins is a Heathen,
And his slaves grow lean and gray,
That he may drink some tepid milk
Exactly twice a day.

THE SONG OF THE STRANGE ASCETIC

Franz Kafka (1883-1924)

There is nothing beside a spiritual work: what we call the world of the senses is Evil in the spiritual world, and what we call evil is only the necessity of a moment in our eternal evolution.

REFLECTIONS

Mikhail Naimy (1889-1988)

What you dislike and cast away as evil is surely liked and picked up by someone, or something as good. Can one thing be at once two self-excluding things? Neither is it the one, nor the other, excepting that your *I* has made it evil; another *I* has made it good.

THE BOOK OF MIRDAD — A LIGHTHOUSE AND A HAVEN

Albert Camus (1913-1960)

I have seen people behave badly with great morality and I note every day that integrity has no need of rules.

THE MYTH OF SISYPHUS

Alan Watts (1915–1973)

At the roots of Chinese life there is a trust in the good-and-evil of one's own nature which is peculiarly foreign to those brought up with the chronic uneasy conscience of the Hebrew-Christian cultures. Yet it was always obvious to the Chinese that a man who mistrusts himself cannot even trust his mistrust, and must therefore be hopelessly confused.

THIS IS IT AND OTHER ESSAYS ON ZEN AND SPIRITUAL EXPERIENCE

Hubert Benoit (1904–1992)

As soon as you have good and evil
Confusion follows and the mind is lost.

THE SUPREME DOCTRINE

HEAVEN
AND HELL

Anonymous

Everyone wants to go to heaven, but no one wants to die.

The Sumerian Underworld

(date unknown, c. 2nd millennium BCE)

It is a house that separates the wicked
and the good; this is a house from out of which
no one escapes, but just men need not fear before its judge,
For in this river of spent souls the good
shall never die although the wicked perish.

SUMERIAN TEXT

Motse (c. 468–401 BCE)

Now, what does Heaven desire and what does it abominate? Heaven desires righteousness and abominates unrighteousness…. But how do we know Heaven desires righteousness and abominates unrighteousness? For, with righteousness the world lives and without it the world dies; with it the world becomes rich and without it the world becomes poor; with it the world becomes orderly and without it the world becomes chaotic. And Heaven likes to have the world live and dislikes to have it die, likes to have it rich and dislikes to have it poor, and likes to have it orderly and dislikes to have it disorderly. Therefore we know Heaven desires righteousness and abominates unrighteousness.

THE WILL OF HEAVEN

Lucretius (99–55 BCE)

I know that men often speak of sickness or of shameful life as more to be dreaded than the terrors of Hell…. But all this talk is based more on a desire to show off than on actual proof, as you may infer from their conduct. These same men, though they may be exiled from home, banished far from the sight of their fellows, soiled with some filthy crime, a prey to every torment, still cling to life.

ON THE NATURE OF THE UNIVERSE

Virgil (70-19 BCE)

Each of us bears his own hell.

AENEID

Saint Augustine (354-430)

But by what means did you make heaven and earth? What tool did you use for this vast work? You did not work as a human craftsman does, making one thing out of something else as his mind directs. His mind can impose upon his material whatever form it perceives within itself by its inner eye. But how could his mind do this unless it was because you had made it?

CONFESSIONS

The Koran (7th Century)

But the true servants of God shall be well provided for,
feasting on fruit, and honored in the gardens of delight.
Reclining face-to-face upon soft couches, they shall be served
with a goblet filled at a gushing fountain, white, and delicious
to those who drink it. It will neither dull their senses nor
befuddle them. They shall sit with bashful, dark-eyed virgins,
as chaste as the sheltered eggs of ostriches.

Sosan (Seng-s'tan)
The Third Zen Patriarch (c. 600)

The perfect Tao knows no difficulties;
It only refuses to make preferences.
When freed from hate and love,
It reveals Itself fully and without disguise.
A tenth of an inch's difference,
And heaven and earth are set apart;
If you want to see It manifest,
Take no thought either for or against it.

ON BELIEVING IN MIND

Argula von Grumbach (c. 1492-1563)

I have even heard some say, "If my father and mother were in hell, I wouldn't want to be in heaven." Not me, not if all my friends were down there.

LETTER TO HER COUSIN, ADAM VON TORRING

Paracelsus (1493-1541)

In every human being there is a special heaven whole and unbroken.

ESSENTIAL WRITINGS

Jacob Böhme (1575-1624)

Where will you seek for God? Seek him in your soul that is proceeded out of the eternal nature, the living fountain of forces wherein the divine working stands.

Oh that I had but the pen of a man, and were able therewith to write down the spirit of knowledge! I can but stammer of great mysteries like a child that is beginning to speak; so very little can the earthly tongue express of that which the spirit comprehends. Yet I will venture to try whether I may incline some to seek the pearl of true knowledge, and myself labor in the works of God in my paradisical garden of roses; for the longing of the eternal nature-mother drives me on to write and to exercise myself in this my knowledge.

No money, nor goods, nor art, nor power can bring you to the eternal rest of the eternal paradise, but only the knowledge in which you may steep your soul. That is the pearl which no thief can steal away; seek after it and you will find the noble treasure…. O beloved man, paradise is the divine Joy. It is the divine and angelical Joy, yet it is not outside the place of this world. When I speak of the fountain and joy of paradise, and of its substance, what it is, I have no similitude for it in this world; I stand in need of angelical speech and knowledge to express it; and though I had them yet I could never express it with this tongue.

THE CONFESSIONS

If we will enter into the kingdom of heaven we must be children, and not cunning and wise in the understanding of this world; we must depart from our earthly reason and enter into obedience to our eternal first Mother. So we shall receive the spirit and live of our Mother, and then also we shall know her habitation.

THE CONFESSIONS

John Milton (1608-1674)

The mind is its own place, and in it self
Can make a Heav'n of Hell, a Hell of Heav'n.

PARADISE LOST

Here we may reign secure, and in my choice
To reign is worth ambition though in hell:
Better to reign in hell, than serve in heav'n.

PARADISE LOST

Robert Browning (1812-1889)

Ah, but a man's reach should exceed his grasp,
Or what's a heaven for?

ANDREA DEL SARTO

Friedrich Wilhelm Nietzsche (1844-1900)

In heaven all the interesting people are missing.

THUS SPAKE ZARATHUSTRA

Evelyn Waugh (1903-1966)

It is a curious thing that every creed promises a paradise which will be absolutely uninhabitable for anyone of civilized taste.

LETTERS

Jean-Paul Sartre (1905-1980)

So that's what Hell is. I'd never have believed it…. Do you remember, brimstone, the stake, the gridiron?…What a joke! No need of a gridiron, Hell is other people.

IN CAMERA

Hubert Benoit (1904-1992)

Everything happens in me as if I believed myself exiled from a paradise which exists somewhere and as if I saw, in such and such a modification of the outside world or of myself, the key capable of opening the door of this lost paradise. And I live in the quest of this key.

   While waiting I kill time as I may.

THE SUPREME DOCTRINE

Sangharakshita (Contemporary)

Heaven, the ultimate goal of so many faiths, since it is a mode of contingent and hence of transitory existence, is accounted no more than a pleasant interlude in a pilgrimage fundamentally of more serious import.

THE THREE JEWELS

IDEALS

Confucius (551–479 BCE)

To be able to practice five things everywhere under heaven
constitutes perfect virtue…gravity, generosity of soul,
sincerity, earnestness, and kindness.

ANALECTS

The superior man goes through his life without any one
preconceived course of action or any taboo. He merely
decides for the moment what is the right thing to do.

THE APHORISMS OF CONFUCIUS, VII,
"THE SUPERIOR MAN AND THE INFERIOR MAN"

Aristotle (384-322 BCE)

So far as in us lies, we must play the immortal and do all in
our power to live by the best element in our nature.

ON INTERPRETATION

Ovid (43 BCE-18 CE)

Thy destiny is only that of man, but thy aspirations may
be those of a god.

ARS AMATORIA

Hsueh-tou (950-1052)

What life can compare to this?
Sitting quietly by the window,
I watch the leaves fall and the flowers bloom,
As the seasons come and go.

UNTITLED

Hakim Sanai (12th Century)

When the eye is pure
it sees purity.

THE WALLED GARDEN OF TRUTH

Mr. Tut-Tut (c. 17th Century)

The sun and moon shoot past like a bullet in our floating
life; only sleep affords a little extension of our span of life.
Business affairs fly about like thick dust to belabor our lives;
only sleep afford a little reprieve. Gorging oneself with fish
and meat morning and night besmirches our taste; only sleep
gives opportunity for a short fast. Contention and strife
disturb our peace; only sleep restores for us a short Golden
Age. As for seeing novel things in our sleep—traveling abroad
and being able to walk without legs and fly without wings—it
provides us also with a little fairyland.

ONE HUNDRED PROVERBS

Charlotte Lennox (c. 1730-1804)

I believe there is an intelligent cause which governs the world
by physical rules. As for moral attributes, there is no such
thing; it is impious and absurd to suppose it.

HENRIETTA

Robert Browning (1812-1889)

Ah, but a man's reach should exceed his grasp,
Or, what's a Heaven for?

LETTERS

Henry Ward Beecher (1813-1887)

We are not to make the ideas of contentment and aspiration
quarrel, for God made them fast friends. A man may aspire, and
yet be quite content until it is time to rise; and both flying and
resting are but parts of one contentment. The very fruit of the
gospel is aspiration. It is to the heart what spring is to the earth,
making every root, and bud, and bough desire to be more.

ROYAL TRUTHS

Carl Schurz (1829-1906)

Ideals are like stars: You will not succeed in touching them
with your hands. But like the seafaring man on the desert
waters, you choose them as your guides, and, following them
you will reach your destiny.

SPEECH

Pierre Teilhard de Chardin (1881-1955)

It will not be long before the human mass closes in upon itself and groups all its members in a definitively realized unity. Respect for one and the same law, one and the same orientation, one and the same spirit, are tending to overlay the permanent diversity of individuals and nations. Wait but a little longer, and we shall form but one solid block. The cement is *setting*.

Already, in the silence of the night, I can hear through this world of tumult a confused rustling as of crystalline needles forming themselves into a pattern or of birds huddling closer together in their nest—a deep murmur of distress, of discomfort, of well-being, of triumph, rising up from the Unity which is reaching its fulfilment.

THE GREAT MONAD

Hazrat Inayat Khan (1882-1927)

The man who has never had an ideal may hope to find one; he is in a better state than the man who allows the circumstances of life to break his ideal. To fall beneath one's ideal is to lose one's track in life; then confusion rises in the mind, and that light which one should hold high becomes covered and obscured, so that it cannot shine out to light one's path.

THE SUFI MESSAGE OF HAZRAT INAYAT KHAN:
THE ART OF PERSONALITY

Robert Bly (Contemporary)

We could say that New Age people in general are addicted to harmony.

IRON JOHN

IMMORTALITY

The Vedas

The gods lived constantly in dread of death—
the might Ender—so with toilsome rites
They worshipped and performed religious acts
Till they became immortal. Then the Ender
Said to the gods, "As ye have made yourselves
Imperishable, so will men endeavor
To free themselves from me; what portion then
Shall I possess in man?" The gods replied,
"Henceforth no being shall become immortal
In his own body; this his mortal frame
Shalt thou still seize; this shall remain thy own.

He who through knowledge or religious works
Henceforth attains to immortality
Shall first present his body, Death, to thee."
SATAPATHA BRAHMANA

The Rig Veda (c. 1200–900 BCE)

See how the dawns have set up their banner in the eastern
half of the sky, adorning and anointing themselves with
sunlight for balm. Unleashing themselves like impetuous
heroes unsheathing their weapons, the tawny cows,
the mothers....

The Upanishads (c. 900–600 BCE)

Above the senses is the mind. Above the mind is the
intellect. Above the intellect is the ego. Above the ego is the
unmanifested seed, the Primal Cause. And verily beyond
the unmanifested seed is the self, the unconditioned knowing
whom one attains to freedom and achieves immortality.

KATHA UPANISHAD

That which dwelling within all things is yet other than all things, which all things do not know whose body is all things, which controls all things from within, He is your own Self, The Inner Controller the Immortal....

BRHAD UPANISHAD

Lao Tzu (c. 6th Century BCE)

Going back to the origin is called peace; it means reversion to destiny. Reversion to destiny is called eternity. He who knows eternity is called enlightened.

TAO TE CHING

Can you hold the door of your tent
Wide to the firmament?
Can you, with the simple stature
Of a child, breathing nature,
Become, notwithstanding,
A man?

TAO TE CHING

Heraclitus (c. 4th Century BCE)

Greater dooms bring greater destinies.

SPEECH

Plato (c. 428-348 BCE)

When the soul returns into itself and reflects, it passes into…
the region of that which is pure and everlasting, immortal
and unchangeable.

PHAEDO

Chuang Tzu (369-286 BCE)

Life and Death, existence and nonexistence, success and
nonsuccess, poverty and wealth, virtue and vice, good and
evil report, hunger and thirst, warmth and cold—these all
revolve upon the changing wheel of Destiny.

Cicero (106-43 BCE)

Whatever that which feels, which has knowledge, which wills,
which has the power of growth, it is celestial and divine, and
for that reason must of necessity be eternal.

TUSCULANAE DISPUTATIONES

Virgil (70–19 BCE)

The great cycle of the ages is renewed. Now the Maiden
returns, returns the Gold Age; a new generation now
descends from heaven.

ECLOGUES

Shankara (788–820)

He who has become liberated in this life gains liberation in
death and is eternally united with Brahman, The Absolute
Reality. Such a seer will never be reborn.

CREST-JEWEL OF DISCRIMINATION

Hakim Sanai (12th Century)

Slave that you are
of fame and shame,
what is eternity to you?

THE WALLED GARDEN OF TRUTH

Meister Eckhart (1260-1327)

The soul is created in a place between Time and Eternity:
with its highest powers it touches Eternity, with its
lower, Time.

Guru Nanak (1469-1539)

Few, some very few,
From this havoc return home,
And others inquire of them
About their lost dear ones.
Many are lost forever,
And weeping and anguish are the lot of those who survive.
Ah, Nanak, how completely helpless mere men are!
It is God's will that is done, for ever and ever.

HYMNS OF GURU NANAK

Jacob Böhme (1575-1624)

I declare unto you that the eternal Being, and also this world,
is like man. Eternity bringeth to birth nothing but that
which is like itself; as you find man to be, just so is eternity.
Consider man in body and soul, in good and evil, in joy and
sorrow, in light and darkness, in power and weakness, in life
and death: all is in man, both heaven and the earth, stars, and
elements; also the threefold God.

THE CONFESSIONS

Henry Vaughan (1622-1695)

I saw Eternity the other night,
Like a great ring of pure and endless light,
All calm, as it was bright;
And round beneath it, Time in hours, days, years,
Driv'n by the spheres
Like a vast shadow mov'd; in which the world
And all her train were hurl'd.

"I SAW ETERNITY THE OTHER NIGHT"

Baruch Spinoza (1632-1677)

It is not possible that we should remember that we existed before our body, for our body can bear no trace of such existence, neither can eternity be defined in terms of time or have any relation to time. But notwithstanding, we feel and know that we are eternal.

TRACTATUS POLITICUS

Thomas Traherne (1636-1674)

Death cannot kill what never dies.

CENTURIES OF MEDITATION

Charlotte Smith (1749-1806)

When the imagination soars into those regions, where the planets pursue each its destined course, in the immensity of space—every planet, probably, containing creatures adapted by the Almighty, to the residence he has placed them in; and when we reflect, that the smallest of these is of as much

consequence in the universe, as this world of ours; how
puerile and ridiculous do those pursuits appear in which we
are so anxiously busied; and how insignificant the trifles
we toil to obtain, or fear to lose.

DESMOND

William Blake (1757-1827)

If the doors of perception were cleansed every thing would
appear to man as it is, infinite.

THE MARRIAGE OF HEAVEN AND HELL

François Guizot (1787-1874)

Neither experience nor science has given man the idea
of immortality.... The idea of immortality rises from the very
depths of his soul—he feels, he sees, he knows that he
is immortal.

GENERAL HISTORY OF CIVILIZATION

Phillips Brooks (1835-1893)

The ideal life is in our blood, and never will be still. We feel the thing we ought to be beating through the thing we are.

PERENNIALS

Sri Ramakrishna (1836-1886)

Infinite is the number of ways leading to the sea of immortality.

It is immaterial how thou gettest into this sea. Suppose there is a reservoir of nectar. It is open to thee to walk slowly down the sloping bank from any point, get to the nectar, and have a drink. Thou gettest immortal in any case.

Again, what doth it signify if one throwest oneself into the reservoir or is pushed into it by somebody? The result in either case is the same. Thou tasteth the nectar—the water of life—in either case. Thou becomest immortal.

HIDDEN TREASURE OF THE GOSPEL OF SRI RAMAKRISHNA, SRI SURATH

Friedrich Wilhelm Nietzsche (1844-1900)

All things return eternally, and ourselves with them; we have already existed in times without number, and all things with us.

QUOTED IN *THE SOUL: AN ARCHEOLOGY*, CLAUDIA SETZER

Charlotte Perkins Gilman (1860-1935)

Eternity is not something that begins after you are dead. It is going on all the time. We are in it now.

THE FORERUNNER

J. Krishnamurti (1895-1986)

To the alone, life is eternal; to the alone there is no death. The alone can never cease to be.

COMMENTARIES ON LIVING—FROM THE NOTEBOOKS OF J. KRISHNAMURTI

John Elof Boodin (1869-1950)

We are material in the hands of the Genius of the universe
for a still larger destiny that we cannot see in the everlasting
rhythm of worlds.

COSMIC EVOLUTION

Carlos Castaneda (1925-1998)

There is nothing more lonely than eternity. And nothing
is more cozy for us than to be a human being. This indeed is
another contradiction—how can man keep the bonds of his
humanness and still venture gladly and purposefully into the
absolute loneliness of eternity?

THE FIRE WITHIN

Norman Cousins (1915-1990)

If something comes to life in others because of you, then you
have made an approach to immortality.

*QUOTED IN THE SOUL: AN ARCHEOLOGY,
CLAUDIA SETZER*

Jacob Neusner (Contemporary)

The idea of life after death is clearly an embarrassment to modern thinking—most major philosophers have ridiculed it—but it is just as clearly the touchstone of all religion. Religion says that being human has eternal meaning. If religion announces that life is over at the grave, then it is not talking about what people expect religion to discuss.

NEWSWEEK, MARCH 27, 1989

JOY AND DESPAIR

The Epic of Gilgamesh (3rd Millennium BCE)

When the gods created man they allotted to him death, but
life they retained in their own keeping. As for you, Gilgamesh,
fill your belly with good things; day and night, night and
day, dance and be merry, feast and rejoice. Let your clothes
be fresh, bathe yourself in water, cherish the little child that
holds your hand, and make your wife happy in your embrace;
for this, too, is the lot of man.

The Bhagavad Gita (c. 500 BCE)

For certain is death for the born,
And certain is birth for the dead;
Therefore over the inevitable
Thou shouldst not grieve.

CHAPTER 2, SECTION 27

The Dhammapada (3rd Century BCE)

O let us live in joy, in love amongst those who hate! Among
  men who hate, let us live in love.
O let us live in joy, in health amongst those who are ill!
  Among men who are ill, let us live in health.

THE PATH OF PERFECTION

Aristotle (384-322 BCE)

True happiness flows from the possession of wisdom and
virtue and not from the possession of external goods.

POLITICS

Mencius (372-289 BCE)

There is no greater delight than to be conscious of sincerity
on self-examination.

BOOK VII

When Heaven is about to confer a great office on any man,
it first exercises his mind with suffering, and his sinews and
bones with toil.

BOOK VI

Menander (c. 342-292 BCE)

Health and intellect are the two blessings of life.

MONOSTIKOI

Epicurus (341-270 BCE)

It is impossible to live pleasurably without living wisely, well,
and justly, and impossible to live wisely, well, and justly
without living pleasurably.

DIOGENES LAERTIUS

Aksapada Gotama (2nd Century BCE)

Misapprehension, faults, activity, birth, and pain, these in
their uninterrupted course constitute the "world." Release,
which consists in the soul's getting rid of the world, is the
condition of supreme felicity marked by perfect tranquillity

and not tainted by any defilement. A person, by the true knowledge of the sixteen categories, is able to remove his misapprehension. When this is done, his faults, viz., affection, aversion and stupidity, disappear. He is then no longer subject to any activity and is consequently freed from transmigration and pains. This is the way in which his release is effected and supreme felicity secured.

THE NYAYA SUTRAS

Shantideva (8th Century)

Having patience I should develop enthusiasm;
For Awakening will dwell only in those who exert themselves.

What is enthusiasm? It is finding joy in what is wholesome.

A GUIDE TO THE BODHISATTVA'S WAY OF LIFE

P'ang Yun (c. 800)

How wondrously supernatural,
And how miraculous this!
I carry water, and I carry fuel.

HAIKU

Ziyad B. al-Arabi (9th Century)

The beginning of ecstasy is the lifting of the veil and
the vision of the Divine Guardian, and the presence of
understanding, and the contemplation of the invisible,
and the discoursing on secret things and perceiving the
nonexistent, and it means that you pass away from where
you are.

WRITINGS

Hroswitha of Gandersheim (c. 935-1000)

Better far that my body should suffer outrage than my soul.

UNTITLED

Milarepa (1040-1123)

I, the sage, am the holy one among men.
I am Milarepa.
I am he who goes his own way;
I am he who has counsel for every circumstance;
I am the sage who has no fixed abode.
I am he who is unaffected whatever befall;
I am the alms-seeker who has no food;
I am the naked man who has no clothes;
I am the beggar who has no possessions.
I am he who takes no thought for the morrow;
I am he who has no house here nor dwelling there;
I am the victor who has known consummation.
I am the madman who counts death happiness;
I am he who has naught and needs naught

THE MESSAGE OF MILAREPA

Héloïse (c. 1098–1164)

The blessings promised us by Christ were not promised to those alone who were priests; woe unto the world, indeed, if all that deserved the name of virtue were shut up in a cloister.

LETTERS

Kabir (c. 1440–1518)

Dance, my heart! Dance today with joy.
The strains of love fill the days and the nights with music,
    and the world is listening to its melodies:
Mad with joy, life and death dance to the rhythm of this
    music. The hills and the sea and the earth dance.
The world of man dances in laughter and tears.
Why put on the robe of the monk, and live aloof from the
    world in lonely pride?
Behold! My heart dances in the delight of a hundred arts;
    and the Creator is well pleased.

ONE HUNDRED POEMS OF KABIR

Michel de Montaigne (1533-1592)

There is indeed a certain sense of gratification when we do a good deed that gives us inward satisfaction, and a generous pride that accompanies a good conscience. A resolutely wicked soul may perhaps arm itself with some assurance, but it cannot provide itself with this contentment and satisfaction…. These testimonies of a good conscience are pleasant; and such a natural pleasure is very beneficial to us; it is the only payment that can never fail.

ESSAYS

Sir Francis Bacon (1561-1626)

What then remains but that we still should cry
For being born, and, being born to die?

THE WORLD

Izaak Walton (1593-1683)

Affliction is a divine diet which though it be not pleasing to mankind, yet almighty God hath often imposed it as a good, though bitter, physic, to those children whose souls are dearest to him.

THE COMPLEATE ANGLER

Mr. Tut-Tut (c. 17th Century)

Poverty is not a disgrace; disgrace lies in poverty without ambition. A mean position is not a cause for contempt; contempt belongs to one in a mean position without ability. Old age is no cause for regret; regret that one is old, having lived in vain. Death is no cause for sorrow; sorrow that one dies without benefit to the world.

ONE HUNDRED PROVERBS

Who does not enjoy his happy moments cannot after all be called lucky; who feels happy in extremities is the real cultivated scholar.

ONE HUNDRED PROVERBS

To be elated at success and disappointed at failure is to be the child of circumstances; how can such a one be called master of himself?

ONE HUNDRED PROVERBS

All people are in financial troubles sometimes. The failure to realize the meaning of poverty must be also considered a fault of the wealthy and successful. Moreover, there are heroes among the poor: the right thing is to open your eyes and broaden your chest.

ONE HUNDRED PROVERBS

John Locke (1632-1704)

The necessity of pursuing true happiness is the foundation of all liberty—Happiness, in its full extent, is the utmost pleasure we are capable of.

LETTERS

Matsuo Basho (1644-1694)

The passing spring,
Birds mourn,
Fishes weep
With tearful eyes.

HAIKU

Matthew Henry (1662-1714)

Extraordinary afflictions are not always the punishment of extraordinary sins, but sometimes the trial of extraordinary graces—Sanctified afflictions are spiritual promotions.

LETTERS

Marie Anne du Deffand (1697-1780)

I remember thinking in my youth that no one was happy but madmen, drunkards, and lovers.

CORRESPONDANCE INÉDITE

Martha Washington (1731-1802)

The greater part of our happiness or misery depends on our dispositions, and not on our circumstances. We carry the seeds of the one or the other about with us in our minds wherever we go.

LETTERS

The Declaration of Independence (July 4th, 1776)

We hold these truths to be self-evident: that all men are created equal; that they are endowed by their Creator with certain inalienable Rights; that among these are Life, Liberty, and the pursuit of Happiness.

Arthur Schopenhauer (1788-1860)

The happiness which we receive from ourselves is greater than that which we obtain from our surroundings.... The world in which a man lives shapes itself chiefly by the way in which he looks at it.

THE WORLD AS WILL AND IDEA

Victor Hugo (1802-1885)

The supreme happiness of life is the conviction that we are loved.

LES MISÉRABLES

Ralph Waldo Emerson (1803-1882)

Nothing can bring you peace but yourself.

Charles Dickens (1812-1870)

Reflect upon your present blessings, of which every man has many; not on your past misfortunes, of which all men have some.

OLIVER TWIST

Robert Louis Stevenson (1850-1894)

There is no duty we so much underrate as the duty of being happy.

LETTERS

George Bernard Shaw (1856-1950)

A lifetime of happiness! No man alive could bear it: It would be hell on earth.

MAN AND SUPERMAN

William Butler Yeats (1865-1939)

I am content to follow to its source
Every event in action or in thought;
Measure the lot; forgive myself the lot!
When such as I cast out remorse
So great a sweetness flows into the breast
We must laugh and we must sing,
We are blest by everything,
Everything we look upon is blessed.

A DIALOGUE OF SELF AND SOUL

Yogaswami (1872-1964)

If you are a king,
Will you have contentment?
If you are a beggar,
Will you have contentment?
Whatever your walk in life may be,
You will only have contentment through
Knowing yourself by yourself.

POSITIVE THOUGHTS FOR DAILY MEDITATION

Happiness and sorrow are twins; let them come and go like clouds.
POSITIVE THOUGHTS FOR DAILY MEDITATION

Winston Churchill (1874-1965)

I am easily satisfied with the very best.
SPEECH

Pope Pius XII (1876-1958)

Our Savior has nowhere promised to make us infallibly happy in this world.
LETTERS

Hazrat Inayat Khan (1882-1927)

Mankind is interdependent, and the happiness of each depends upon the happiness of all, and it is this lesson that humanity has to learn today as the first and the last lesson.
*THE SUFI MESSAGE OF HAZRAT INAYAT KHAN:
THE ART OF PERSONALITY*

Robert Lynd (1892-1970)

I am a confirmed believer in blessings in disguise. I prefer them undisguised when I myself happen to be the person blessed; in fact I can hardly recognize a blessing in disguise except when it is bestowed upon someone else.

MIDDLETOWN

J. Krishnamurti (1895-1986)

There is great happiness in not wanting, in not being something, in not going somewhere.

COMMENTARIES ON LIVING – FROM THE NOTEBOOKS OF J. KRISHNAMURTI

To seek fulfilment is to invite frustration.

COMMENTARIES ON LIVING – FROM THE NOTEBOOKS OF J. KRISHNAMURTI

Lillian Hellman (1905-1984)

I am suspicious of guilt in myself and in other people; it is usually a way of not thinking, or of announcing one's own fine sensibilities the better to be rid of them fast.

LETTERS

Albert Camus (1913-1960)

For the first time, the first, I laid my heart open to the benign indifference of the universe. To feel it so like myself, indeed so brotherly, made me realize that I'd been happy, and that I was happy still.

THE MYTH OF SISYPHUS

Alan Watts (1915-1973)

Not only the anxiety but also the sheer stalemate and paralysis which often attend strictly intelligent and non-instinctual action are the most important causes of anti-intellectual movements in our society. It is through impatience and exasperation with such snarls that democracies vote themselves into dictatorships. It is in protest against the laborious unmanageability of vast technical knowledge in literature, painting, and music that writers and artists go berserk and break every rule in the name of sheer instinctual exuberance. It is in revolt against the insufferable heaps of unproductive paperwork that small businesses sell out to big corporations, and independent professional men take routine salaried jobs without responsibility. It is in disgust with the complex organization of the omnipotent registrar's office and the unimaginative pedantry of the Ph.D. course that people of real genius or creative ability are increasingly unable to work in our universities. It is also in despair of being able to understand or make any productive contribution to the highly organized chaos of our politico-economic system that large numbers of people simply abandon political and social commitments. They just let society be taken over by a pattern of organization which is as self-proliferative as a weed, and whose ends and values are neither human nor instinctual but mechanical. And we should note that a self-contradictory system of action breeds forms of revolt which are contradictory among themselves.

THIS IS IT: AND OTHER ESSAYS ON ZEN AND SPIRITUAL EXPERIENCE

Osho (1931-1990)

And the miracle is: If you can go into your suffering as a meditation, watching, to the deepest roots of it, just through watching, it disappears. You don't have to do anything more than watching. If you have found the authentic cause by your watching, the suffering will disappear.

DISCOURSES

William Bennett (Contemporary)

Happiness is like a cat. If you try to coax it or call it, it will avoid you, it will never come. But if you pay no attention to it and go about your business, you'll find it rubbing against your legs and jumping into your lap.

QUOTED IN *THE SOUL: AN ARCHEOLOGY*, CLAUDIA SETZER

Carlos Castaneda (1925-1998)

Modern man has left the realm of the unknown and the mysterious, and has settled down in the realm of the functional. He has turned his back to the world of the foreboding and the exulting and has welcomed the world of boredom.

THE FIRE WITHIN

Rabbi Harold Kushner (Contemporary)

When your life is filled with the desire to see the holiness in everyday life, something magical happens: ordinary life becomes extraordinary, and the very process of life begins to nourish your soul!

GOD'S FINGERPRINTS ON THE SOUL, HANDBOOK FOR THE SOUL, EDS. RICHARD CARLSON AND BENJAMIN SHIELD

Bernard Levin (1928-2004)

Countries like ours are full of people who have all of the material comforts they desire, yet lead lives of quiet (and at times noisy) desperation, understanding nothing but the fact that there is a hole inside them and that however much food and drink they pour into it, however many motorcars and television sets they stuff it with, however many well-balanced children and loyal friends they parade around the edges of it…it aches!

THE TIMES (LONDON), 1968

Sogyal Rinpoche (Contemporary)

May the vision that so many mystic masters of all traditions have had, of a future world free of cruelty and horror, where humanity can live in the ultimate happiness of the nature of mind, come, through all our efforts, to be realized.

THE TIBETAN BOOK OF LIVING AND DYING

Rosemary Radford Ruether
(Contemporary)

A reencounter with original blessing is experienced as a leap to a new state of being that breaks the hold of false power upon our spirit. In this sense, it is psychologically experienced as something beyond our present state of existence. But…we know it to be the most natural thing in the world, since, when we encounter original blessing, we immediately recognize, it as our true selves—something with which we are already gifted, not something we have to strive to achieve.

QUOTED FROM *THE SOUL: AN ARCHEOLOGY*,
CLAUDIA SETZER

Bernie Siegel (Contemporary)

Every day is my best day; this is my life; I'm not going to have this moment again.

LOVE: THE WORK OF THE SOUL, HANDBOOK FOR THE SOUL, EDS. RICHARD CARLSON & BENJAMIN SHIELD

D. T. Suzuki (1870-1966)

The ultimate standpoint of Zen…is that we have been led astray through ignorance to find a split in our own being, that there was from the very beginning no need for a struggle between the finite and the infinite, that the peace we are seeking so eagerly after has been there all the time.

QUOTED FROM *THE SOUL: AN ARCHEOLOGY*, CLAUDIA SETZER

Thomas Szasz (Contemporary)

Happiness is an imaginary condition formerly often attributed by the living to the dead, now usually attributed by adults to children, and by children to adults.

"EMOTIONS" IN *THE SECOND SIN*

KNOWLEDGE

Confucius (551–479 BCE)

To know what you know and know what you don't know is the characteristic of one who knows.

THE APHORISMS OF CONFUCIUS, V, "WIT AND WISDOM"

The young people should be good sons at home, polite and respectful in society; they should be careful in their conduct and faithful, love the people, and associate themselves with the kind people. If after learning all this, they still have energy left, let them read books.

THE APHORISMS OF CONFUCIUS, X, "ON EDUCATION, RITUAL AND POETRY"

Chuang Tzu (369-286 BCE)

For we can only know that we know nothing, and a little knowledge is a dangerous thing.

QUOTED IN THE SOUL: AN ARCHEOLOGY,
CLAUDIA SETZER

Cherish that which is within you, and shut off that which is without; for much knowledge is a curse.

ON TOLERANCE

Human life is limited, but knowledge is limitless. To drive the limited in pursuit of the limitless is fatal; and to presume that one really knows is fatal indeed!

THE PRESERVATION OF LIFE

Hakim Sanai (12th Century)

But how will you ever know him [God],
as long as you are unable to know yourself?

THE WALLED GARDEN OF TRUTH

He doesn't know his own self:
how should he know the self of another?
THE WALLED GARDEN OF TRUTH

If you know your own worth,
what need you care about
the acceptance or rejection of others?
THE WALLED GARDEN OF TRUTH

Knowing what you know,
be serene also, like a mountain;
and do not be distressed by misfortune.
Knowledge without serenity
is an unlit candle;
together they are honeycomb;
honey without wax is a noble thing;
wax without honey is only fit for burning.
THE WALLED GARDEN OF TRUTH

Farid ud-Din Attar (c. 1120-1193)

You cannot carve your way to heaven's throne
If you sit locked in vanity alone.
You need a skillful guide; you cannot start
This ocean-voyage with blindness in your heart.

THE CONFERENCE OF THE BIRDS

Michel de Montaigne (1533-1592)

The active pursuit of truth is our proper business. We have
no excuse for conducting it badly or unfittingly. But failure
to capture our prey is another matter. For we are born to
quest after it; to possess it belongs to a greater power. Truth
is not, as Democritus said, hidden in the depths of the
abyss, but situated rather at an infinite height in the divine
understanding. The world is but a school of inquiry.

ESSAYS

It once pleased me to see, in one place or another, men who had, in the name of religion, made vows of ignorance as well as of chastity, poverty, and penitence. This, too, is a gelding of our unruly appetites, a blunting of that cupidity which drives us on to the study of books, and a ridding the mind of that luxuriant complacency which tickles us with the belief in our learning. And it is a rich fulfilment of the view of worldly poverty to add to it poverty of mind. We need hardly any knowledge to live happily.

ESSAYS

Sir Francis Bacon (1561-1626)

Knowledge is power.

MEDITATIONES SACRAE DE HAERESIBUS

Alfred, Lord Tennyson (1809-1892)

Knowledge comes, but wisdom lingers.

MOTTO

Shivapuri Baba (1826-1963)

There is a vast difference in knowing a thing and in having it. Knowledge of a thing is not necessarily the realization of it. For instance, we know that there is such a country as England which is so and so. But this knowledge itself is not the realization of it. Likewise, for a real aspirant after truth, the simple knowledge gained of it alone can do no good. Such a knowledge we can have from the writings of the great thinkers of the world, the Vedas and the Upanishads. Suppose we have gone through all of them and gained knowledge of the truth, does this mean that we have realized it? Yes, we have done what we can to gain the knowledge. But with simply this we do not get satisfied. We can still assume that there is something beyond and there is a longing for that.

QUOTED *IN LONG PILGRIMAGE*, J. G. BENNETT

Mary Coleridge (1861-1907)

The fruits of the tree of knowledge are various; he must be strong indeed who can digest all of them.

*GATHERED LEAVES FOR THE PROSE OF
MARY E. COLERIDGE*

Hermann Hesse (1877-1962)

Knowledge can be communicated, but not wisdom. One can find it, live it, be fortified by it, do wonders through it, but one cannot communicate and teach it.

SIDDHARTHA

Lillian Smith (1897-1966)

To believe in something not yet proved and to underwrite it without lives: It is the only way we can keep the future open. Man, surrounded by facts, permitting himself no surprise, no intuitive flash, no great hypothesis, no risk, is in a locked cell. Ignorance cannot seal the mind and imagination more securely.

THE JOURNEY

Osho (1931-1990)

Knowledge is always borrowed. It is not a flower that grows in your soul, it is something plastic that been imposed upon you.

DISCOURSES

Carlos Castaneda (1925-1998)

In the face of the unknown, man is adventurous. It is a quality of the unknown to give us a sense of hope and happiness. Man feels robust, exhilarated. Even the apprehension that it arouses is very fulfilling…. [But] whenever what is taken to be the unknown turns out to be the unknowable the results are disastrous…for the unknowable has no energizing effects whatsoever. It is not within human reach; therefore, it should not be intruded upon foolishly or even prudently.

THE FIRE WITHIN

LIFE

The Charvaka, from the Brhaspati Sutra

While life is yours, live joyously;
None can escape Death's searching eye:
When once this frame of ours they burn,
How shall it e'er again return?

A SOURCE BOOK IN INDIAN PHILOSOPHY,
S. RADHAKRISHNAN AND CHARLES A. MOORE

Lao Tzu (c. 6th Century BCE)

Existence is beyond the power of words
To define:
Terms may be used
But are none of them absolute.

TAO TE CHING

Fatalism is acceptance of destiny
And to accept destiny is to face life with open eyes,
Whereas not to accept destiny is to face death blindfold.

TAO TE CHING

The way to use life is to do nothing through acting,
The way to use life is to do everything through being.

TAO TE CHING

Let life ripen and then fall.
Will is not the way at all:
Deny the way of life and you are dead.

TAO TE CHING

The Golden Mean of Tsesze
(c. 4th Century BCE)

Confucius remarked: "There are men who seek for the
abstruse and strange and live a singular life in order that they
may leave a name to posterity. This is what I never would do.
There are again good men who try to live in conformity with

the moral law, but who, when they have gone halfway, throw it up. I never could give it up. Lastly, there are truly moral men who unconsciously live a life in entire harmony with the universal moral order and who live unknown to the world and unnoticed of men without any concern. It is only men of holy, divine natures who are capable of this."

THE GOLDEN MEAN

The Dhammapada (3th Century BCE)

Look upon the man who tells thee thy faults as if he told thee of a hidden treasure, the wise man who shows thee the dangers of life. Follow that man: He who follows him will see good and not evil.

THE PATH OF PERFECTION

What is life but the flower or the fruit which falls when ripe, but yet which ever fears the untimely frost?

THE PATH OF PERFECTION

Wang Wei (699-761)

The world's affairs and the floating clouds—
> why question them?
You had best take life easily—
> and have a good dinner

"GIVING P'EI TI A DRINK," IN *THE POEMS OF WANG WEI*

Omar Khayyam (d. 1123)

For in and out, above, about, below,
'Tis nothing but a Magic Shadow-show,
Play'd in a Box whose Candle is the Sun,
Round which we Phantom Figures come and go.

RUBAIYAT

Hildegarde von Bingen (1098-1179)

I am that supreme and fiery force that sends forth all
living sparks. Death hath no part in me, yet I bestow death,
wherefore I am girt about with wisdom as with wings. I am
that living and fiery essence of the divine substance that
glows in the beauty of the fields, and in the shining water,

and in the burning sun and the moon and the stars, and in
the force of the invisible wind, the breath of all living things, I
breathe in the green grass and in the flowers, and in the living
waters…All these live and do not die because I am in them.…
I am the source of the thundered word by which all creatures
were made, I permeate all things that they may not die.
I am life.

MEDITAITONS

Jalal al-Din Rumi (1207-1273)
The breath of the flute player,
does it belong to the flute?

TALES OF THE MATHNAWI

Guru Nanak (1469-1539)
Were life's span extended to the four ages
And ten times more,
Were one known over the nine shores
Ever in humanity's fore,
Were one to achieve greatness

With a name noised over the earth,
If one found not favor with the lord
What would it all be worth?

HYMNS OF GURU NANAK

Michel de Montaigne (1533-1592)

Our life, like the harmony of the world, is composed of
contrarieties, also of varying tones, sweet and harsh, sharp
and flat, soft and loud. If a musician liked one sort only, what
effect would he make? He must be able to employ them
together and blend them. And we, too, must accept the good
and evil that are consubstantial with our life. Our existence
is impossible without this mixture, and one side is no less
necessary to us than the other.

ESSAYS

Sir Francis Bacon (1561-1626)

But men must know that in this theater of man's life, it is
reserved only for God and angels to be lookers on.

THE ADVANCEMENT OF LEARNING

John Donne (1572-1631)

Though our natural life were no life, but rather a continual dying, yet we have two lives besides that, an eternal life reserved for heaven, but yet a heavenly life, too, a spiritual life, even in this world.

QUOTED IN *THE SOUL: AN ARCHEOLOGY*,
CLAUDIA SETZER

Mr. Tut-Tut (c. 17th Century)

To see through fame and wealth is to gain a little rest; to see through life and death is to gain a big rest.

ONE HUNDRED PROVERBS

Sir Thomas Browne (1605-1682)

Life is a pure flame, and we live by an invisible sun within us.

QUOTED IN *THE SOUL: AN ARCHEOLOGY*,
CLAUDIA SETZER

William Blake (1757–1827)

For man has closed himself up, 'till he sees all things thro' the chinks of his cavern.

THE PORTABLE BLAKE

John Stuart Mill (1806–1873)

Human existence is girt round with mystery: The narrow region of our experience is a small island in the midst of a boundless sea.

THREE ESSAYS ON RELIGION

Mary Baker Eddy (1821–1910)

To live and let live, without clamor for distinction of recognition; to wait on divine Love; to write truth first on the tablet of one's own heart—this is the sanity and perfection of living, and my human ideal.

MESSAGE TO THE MOTHER CHURCH

Annie Besant (1847-1933)

We are part of one great Life, which knows no failure, no loss of effort or strength, which "mightily and sweetly ordering all things" bears the world onwards to their goal.

QUOTED IN *THE SOUL: AN ARCHEOLOGY*, CLAUDIA SETZER

Vincent van Gogh (1853-1890)

First of all the twinkling stars vibrated, but remained motionless in space, then all the celestial globes were united into one series of movements…. Firmament and planets both disappeared, but the mighty breath which gives lives to all things and in which all is bound up remained.

LETTERS

George Santayana (1863-1952)

There is no cure for birth and death save to enjoy the interval.

Natsume Soseki (1867-1916)

What a long spring day!
Catching yawns from one another
We go each our way.

KOAN

William Henry Davies (1871-1940)

What is this life if, full of care,
We have no time to stand and stare?

COLLECTED POEMS

G. I. Gurdjieff (1877-1949)

Each of them (our inner selves) is a caliph for an hour, does what he likes regardless of everything, and, later on, the others have to pay for it. And there is no order among them whatever. Whoever gets the upper hand is master. He whips everyone on all sides and takes heed of nothing. But the next moment another sees the whip and beats him. Imagine a country where everyone can be king for five minutes and do during these five minutes just what he likes with the whole kingdom. That is our life.

IN SEARCH OF THE MIRACULOUS: FRAGMENTS OF AN UNKNOWN TEACHING, P.D. OUSPENSKY

Hermann Hesse (1877-1962)

It is harder to kill something that is spiritually alive than it is to bring the dead back to life.

SIDDHARTHA

Pierre Teilhard de Chardin (1881-1955)

And then there is the man who picks himself up, covered in dust but unharmed, after a five-nine has exploded uncomfortably close to him: Whence comes this joyful expansion of the heart, this alacrity of the will, this new savor in life—things that we do not experience if we have just missed being run over by a train or shot by a bullet from a carelessly handled revolver? Is it solely the joy of 'staying alive' that so fills the soul of survivors in wartime and gives new youth to their world? For my part, I believe that the completely fresh flavor added to living after a narrow escape derives above all from this deep-seated intuition that the existence we have found again, consecrated by danger, is a new existence. The physical well-being which at that moment spreads over the soul is a sign of the higher Life into which the survivor has just been baptized. The man who has passed through the fire is another species of man among men.

NOSTALGIA FOR THE FRONT

P. G. Wodehouse (1881-1975)

I spent the afternoon musing on Life. If you come to think of it, what a queer thing Life is! So unlike anything else, don't you know, if you see what I mean.

MY MAN JEEVES

D. H. Lawrence (1885-1930)

For man, the vast marvel is to be alive. For man, as for flower and beast and bird, the supreme triumph is to be most vividly, most perfectly alive. Whatever the unborn and the dead may know, they cannot know the beauty, the marvel of being alive in the flesh. The dead may look after the afterward. But the magnificent here and now of life in the flesh is ours, and ours alone and ours only for a time. We ought to dance with rapture that we should be alive and in the flesh, and part of the living incarnate cosmos. I am part of the sun as my eye is part of me. That I am part of the earth my feet know perfectly, and my blood is part of the sea. My soul knows that I am part of the human race, my soul is an organic part of the great human soul, as my spirit is part of my nation. In my very own self, I am part of my family. There is nothing of me that is alone and absolute except my mind, and we shall find that the mind has no existence by itself, it is only the glitter of the sun on the surface of the waters.

APOCALYPSE

Paul Tillich (1886-1965)

We are separated from the mystery, the depth, and the greatness of our existence. We hear the voice of that depth; but our ears are closed.

THE SHAKING OF THE FOUNDATIONS

T. S. Eliot (1888-1965)

Let us go, through certain half-deserted streets,
The muttering retreats
Of restless nights in one-night cheap hotels
And sawdust restaurants with oyster shells:
Streets that follow like a tedious argument
Of insidious intent

In the room the women come and go
Talking of Michelangelo.
THE LOVE SONG OF J. ALFRED PRUFROCK

Eugene O'Neill (1888-1953)

Life is perhaps best regarded as a bad dream between
two awakenings.
*QUOTED IN THE SOUL: AN ARCHEOLOGY,
CLAUDIA SETZER*

Mikhail Naimy (1889-1988)

Die to live, or live to die.
THE BOOK OF MIRDAD—A LIGHTHOUSE AND A HAVEN

Let things alone and labor not to change them. For they seem what they seem only because you seem what you seem. They neither see nor speak except you lend them sight and speech.

THE BOOK OF MIRDAD—A LIGHTHOUSE AND A HAVEN

Albert Camus (1913-1960)

I see many people die because they judge that life is not worth living. I see others paradoxically getting killed for the ideas or illusions that give them a reason for living (what is called a reason for living is also an excellent reason for dying). I therefore conclude that the meaning of life is the most urgent of questions.

THE MYTH OF SISYPHUS

But the point is to live.

THE MYTH OF SISYPHUS

If any art is devoid of lessons, it is certainly music. It is too closely related to mathematics not to have borrowed their gratuitousness. That game the mind plays with itself according to set and measured laws takes place in the sonorous compass that belongs us and beyond which the vibrations nevertheless meet in an inhuman universe. There is no purer sensation.

THE MYTH OF SISYPHUS

Alan Watts (1915-1973)

To be a Tathagata is to dance the day instead of working it. The "curse of work" that came from the Fall was the supposition that one "must" live.

THE BOOK: ON THE TABOO AGAINST KNOWING WHO YOU ARE

A bird is one egg's way of becoming other eggs.

THE BOOK: ON THE TABOO AGAINST KNOWING WHO YOU ARE

Osho (1931-1990)

Life is not short; life is eternal, so there is no question of any hurry. By hurrying you can only miss. In existence do you see any hurry? Seasons come in their time, flowers come in their time, trees are not running to grow fast because life is short. It seems as if the whole existence is aware of the eternity of life.

We have been here always, and we will be here always— of course not in the same forms, and not in the same bodies. Life goes on evolving, reaching to higher stages. But there is no end anywhere, and there has been no beginning anywhere either.

DISCOURSES

The first thing to be done is laughter, because that sets the trend for the whole day. If you wake up laughing, you will soon begin to feel how absurd life is. Nothing is serious: Even your disappointments are laughable, even your pain is laughable, even you are laughable.

THE ORANGE BOOK

Alan Bennett (Contemporary)

You know life…it's rather like opening a tin of sardines.
We are all of us looking for the key.

BEYOND THE FRINGE

Sam Keen (Contemporary)

Once we abandon the age-old quest for consistency, for
forging a single identity, for a unifying vision, we are left
with no guiding principle except to follow the dictates of
the moment.

FIRE IN THE BELLY

The Mother (1878-1973)

The number of suggestions one could call "defeatist" within
the earth's atmosphere is simply overwhelming! It's so
surprising that everything isn't crushed to death…. Everyone
is constantly creating disasters; expecting the worst, seeing
the worst, observing only the worst…. And it's down to the
smallest things, you know (the body observes everything).
When people react harmoniously, everything goes well;

when there is the reaction which I now call defeatist: If the person picks up an object, he drops it. It happens all the time, without any reason whatsoever; it's the presence of that defeatist consciousness. And I've seen this: All the wills or vibrations (for in the end, it all boils down to qualities of vibration) that bring about everything, from little nuisances to the greatest disasters, all have that same quality!

SATPREM, THE MIND OF THE CELLS

U. G. Krishnamurti (Contemporary)

The natural state is not the state of self-realized or God-realized man, it is not a thing to be achieved or attained, it is not a thing to be willed into existence; it is there—it is the living state. This state is just the functional activity of life. By "life" I do not mean something abstract; it is the life of the senses, functioning naturally without the interference of thought. Thought is an interloper, which thrusts itself into the affairs of the senses. It has a profound motive; thought directs the activity of the senses to get something out of them, and uses them to give continuity to itself. This constant demand to experience everything is because if we don't, we come to an end—that is, the "we" as we know ourselves and we don't want that at all. What we want is the continuity.

THE MYSTIQUE OF ENLIGHTENMENT—THE
UNRATIONAL IDEAS OF A MAN CALLED U. G.

Leonard Lauder (Contemporary)

When a person with experience meets a person with money, the person with experience will get the money. And the person with the money will get some experience.

ON THE EARLY YEARS OF THE ESTEE LAUDER COMPANY,
WOMAN'S ECONOMIC DEVELOPMENT CORPORATION,
FEBRUARY 1985

Rupert Sheldrake (Contemporary)

Spoken softly, the possibility is open that the phenomenon of "life" depends upon laws and factors which have not been recognized so far by scientists.

A NEW SCIENCE OF LIFE

Marion Woodman (Contemporary)

We all experience "soul moments" in life—when we see a magnificent sunrise, hear the call of a loon, see the wrinkles in our mother's hands, or smell the sweetness of a bay. During these moments, our body, as well as our brain, resonates as we experience the glory of being a human being.

SOUL MOMENTS: HANDBOOK FOR THE SOUL,
EDS. RICHARD CARLSON & BENJAMIN SHIELD

Gary Zukav (Contemporary)

As the human species awakens to itself as a collection of immortal souls learning together, caring for the environment and the earth will become a matter of the heart, the natural response of souls moving toward their full potential.

EVOLUTION AND BUSINESS

LOVE

Greek Proverb
The heart that loves is always young.

Lao Tzu (c. 6th century BCE)
He who loves the world as his body may be entrusted with
the empire.

TAO TE CHING

Confucius (551–479 BCE)
Can there be a love which does not make demands
on its object?

ANALECTS

Sophocles (c. 496–406 BCE)

One word frees us of all the weight and pain of life:
That word is love.

OEDIPUS AT COLONUS

Euripides (480–406 BC)

Love is all we have, the only way that each can help the other.

ORESTES

Plato (c. 428–348 BCE)

[Love is] the joy of the good, the wonder of the wise, the amazement of the gods.

THE SYMPOSIUM

Menander (c. 342–292 BCE)

Love blinds all men alike, both the reasonable and the foolish.

ANDRIA

Lucretius (99–55 BCE)

Love is a product of habit.

DE RERUM NATURA

Virgil (70-19 BCE)

Love conquers all: and let us, too, surrender to love.

ECLOGUES

Ovid (43 BCE-17 CE)

Love is a kind of warfare.

ARS AMATORIA

Old Testament

Hatred stirs up strife, but love covers all offenses.

PROVERBS 10:12

Thou shalt love thy neighbor as thyself.

LEVITICUS 19:18

New Testament

I may have all knowledge and understand all secrets; I may have all the faith needed to move mountains—but if I have no love, I am nothing.

I CORINTHIANS, 13, 11

Be kindly affectioned one to another with brotherly love:
in honor preferring one another.

ROMANS 12:10

Tacitus (c. 55-117)

It is human to hate those whom we have injured.

LIFE OF AGRICOLA

Epictetus (55-135)

The universe is but one great city, full of beloved ones, divine
and human by nature, endeared to each other.

MANUAL

The Mishna (c. 200)

Ben Azai used to say: "Despise no man, and consider
nothing impossible, for every man has his hour and
everything its place."

*THE TALMUD QUOTED IN THE WORLD'S GREAT
SCRIPTURES, LEWIS BROWNE*

Saint Augustine (354-430)

There is no one in the whole human family to whom kindly affection is not due by reason of the bond of a common humanity, although it may not be due on the ground of reciprocal love.

TO PROBA

Boethius (c. 470-524)

Who can give law to lovers? Love is a greater law to itself.

DE CONSOLATIONE PHILOSOPHIAE

Shantideva (8th Century)

There is no evil like hatred,
And no fortitude like patience.

A GUIDE TO THE BODHISATTVA'S WAY OF LIFE

Al-Ghazali (b. 1058)

Love for God is the farthest reach of all stations, the sun of the highest degrees, and there is no station after that of love, except its fruit and its consequences.

*QUOTED FROM THE SOUL: AN ARCHAEOLOGY,
CLAUDIA SETZER*

Hakim Sanai (12th Century)

Whilst in this land
of fruitless pursuits,
you are always unbalanced, always
either all back or all front;
but once the seeking soul has progressed
just a few paces beyond this state,
loves seizes the reins.

THE WALLED GARDEN OF TRUTH

Love's conqueror is he
whom love conquers.

THE WALLED GARDEN OF TRUTH

Farid ud-Din Attar (c. 1120-1193)

A man whose eyes love opens risks his soul—
His dancing breaks beyond the mind's control.

THE CONFERENCE OF THE BIRDS

Mechtild von Magdeburg (1207-1249)

Those who would know much, and love little, will ever remain at but the beginning of a godly life.

THE FLOWING LIGHT OF THE GODHEAD

Jalal al-Din Rumi (1207-1273)

Love makes bitter things sweet; love converts base copper to gold. By love dregs become clear; by love pains become healing. By love the dead is brought to life; by love a king is made a slave.

TALES OF THE MASNAVI

I have ordained for every man a manner of conduct; I have given to every man his own way of expression. In regard to him it is praiseworthy, in regard to you it is blameworthy; in regard to him it is honey, in regard to you it is poison. I am independent of all purity and uncleanness; I am far above all sloth and alacrity. I made not any commandment that I might make profit, but I might be bountiful to My servants. To Indians the usage of Hind is praiseworthy, to Sindians the usage of Sind is praiseworthy; I am not sanctified by their magnificats, it is they who are sanctified so that they scatter pearls. I do not regard the tongue and the speech; I regard the inward soul and the spirit's state. I look into the heart, whether it be humble even though the words spoken be far from humble. For the heart is the substance; speech is only the accident; therefore the accident is adventitious, the substance is the true object. How many more of these phrases, these concepts, these metaphors? What I want is burning, burning; attune yourself to burning! Kindle a fire of love in your soul, burn utterly all thought and expression!

TALES OF THE MASNAVI

Geoffrey Chaucer (c. 1343-1400)

Love is blind.

"THE MERCHANT'S TALE," IN *THE CANTERBURY TALES*

Catherine of Siena (1347-1380)

If thou wish to reach the perfection of love, it befits thee to set thy life in order.

LETTER TO MONNA ALESSA DEI SARACINI

Thomas à Kempis (1380-1471)

Love is swift, sincere, pious, pleasant, generous, strong,
patient, faithful, prudent, long-suffering, manly, and never
seeking her own; for wheresoever a man seeketh his own,
there he falleth from love.

IMITATION OF CHRIST

Jami (1414-1492)

Two sages had taken up the topic of love.

One declared: "The hallmarks of love are misfortune
and suffering. Incessantly the lover experiences torment
and affliction."

The other replied, "Enough! I suppose you have never
seen peace follow war, or tasted the delight of union after
separation! None in the world are more delightful than those
who, with a pure heart, give themselves to love; and none
cruder than those insensitive beings who remain aloof from
such cares!"

THE ABODE OF SPRING

Kabir (c. 1440-1518)

Knowing nothing shuts the iron gates; the new love
opens them.
The sound of the gates opening wakes the beautiful
woman asleep.
Kabir says: Fantastic! Don't let a chance like this go by!

THE FISH IN THE SEA IS NOT THIRSTY

Mira Bai (c. 1498-1546)

I am mad with love
And no one understands my plight.
Only the wounded
Understand the agonies of the wounded,
When a fire rages in the heart.

HYMNS OF PRAISE: DEVOTIONAL POEMS

Marina de Guevara (c. 1510-1559)

To bring the heart into tune with God is better than audible prayer.

LETTERS

Saint John of the Cross (1542-1591)

The very fire of love which afterward is united with the soul, glorifying it, is that which previously assails it by purging it, just as the fire that penetrates a log of wood is the same that first makes an assault upon it, wounding it with its flame, drying it out, and stripping it of its unsightly qualities until it is so disposed that it can be penetrated and transformed into the fire.

THE ASCENT OF MOUNT CARMEL

John Lyly (c. 1553-1606)

Love knoweth no laws.

EUPHUES

Sir Francis Bacon (1561-1626)

It is impossible to love and be wise.

OF LOVE

Christopher Marlowe (1564-1593)

Who ever loved that loved not at first sight?

HERO AND LEANDER

William Shakespeare (1564-1616)

Let me not to the marriage of true minds
Admit impediments.
Love is not love
Which alters when it alteration finds,
Or bends with the remover to remove.
Oh no! It is an ever-fixed mark
That looks on tempests and is never shaken.
It is the star to every wandering bark,
Whose worth's unknown, although his height be taken.

SONNET 116

Love is a familiar. Love is a devil. There is no evil angel
but Love.

LOVE'S LABOUR'S LOST, I, 2

But love is blind, and lovers cannot see
The pretty follies that themselves commit.

THE MERCHANT OF VENICE, II, 6

The course of true love never did run smooth.

A MIDSUMMER NIGHT'S DREAM, I, 1

Speak of me as I am...one that loved not wisely but too well.

OTHELLO, V, 2

They do not love that do not show their love.

THE TWO GENTLEMEN OF VERONA, I, 2

John Donne (1572-1631)

Love, all alike, no season knows, nor clime,
Nor hours, days, months, which are the rags of time.

THE SUN RISING

Ben Jonson (c. 1572-1637)

Who falls for love of God shall rise a star.

LETTERS

Jacob Böhme (1575-1624)

O gracious amiable Blessedness and great Love, how sweet art thou! How friendly and courteous art thou! How pleasant and lovely is thy relish and taste! How ravishing sweetly dost thou smell! O noble Light, and bright Glory, who can apprehend thy exceeding beauty? How comely adorned is thy love! How curious and excellent are thy colors! And all this eternally. Who can express it?

Or why and what do I write, whose tongue does but stammer like a child which is learning to speak? With what shall I compare it? Or to what shall I liken it? Shall I compare it with the love of this world? No, that is but a mere dark valley to it.

O immense Greatness! I cannot compare thee with any thing, but only with the resurrection from the dead; there will the Love-Fire rise up again in us, and rekindle again our astringent, bitter, and cold, dark and dead powers, and embrace us most courteously and friendly.

O gracious, amiable, blessed Love and clear bright Light, tarry with us, I pray thee, for the evening is at hand.

THE CONFESSIONS

Thomas Fuller (1608-1661)

Malice drinketh up the greater part of its own poison.

François La Rochefoucauld (1613-1680)

There is no disguise which can hide love for long where it exists, or simulate it where it does not.

MAXIMS

If one judges love by the majority of its effects, it is more like hatred than friendship.

MAXIMS

Molière (1622-1673)

We are easily duped by those we love.

TARTUFFE

John Dryden (1631-1700)

For heaven be thanked, we live in such an age,
When no man dies for love, but on the stage.

EPILOGUE TO MITHRIDATES

John Gay (1685-1732)

She who has never loved has never lived.

CAPTIVES

Voltaire (1694-1778)

Love those who love you.

LETTER TO D'ALEMBERT, NOVEMBER 28, 1762

Ba'al Shem Tov (1700-1760)

From every human being there rises a light that reaches straight to heaven, and when two souls that are destined to be together find each other, the streams of light flow together and a single brighter light goes forth from that united being.

PRAYER

Samuel Johnson (1709-1784)

I am willing to love all mankind, "except an American."

JAMES BOSWELL, LIFE OF JOHNSON

Pierre-Augustin de Beaumarchais (1732-1799)

Where love is concerned, too much is not even enough.

THE MARRIAGE OF FIGARO

Sébastien R. N. Chamfort (1740-1794)

Love, such as it is in society, is only the exchange of two fantasies, and the contact of two bodies.

MAXIMES ET PENSÉES

William Blake (1756-1827)

Love seeketh not itself to please,
Nor for itself hath any care,
But for another gives its ease,
And builds a Heaven in Hell's despair.

UNTITLED

Love seeketh only Self to please,
To bind another to its delight,
Joys in another's loss of ease,
And builds a Hell in Heaven's despite.
UNTITLED

J. C. Friedrich von Schiller (1759–1805)

What is life without the radiance of love?
WALLENSTEIN'S DEATH

Germaine de Staël (1766–1817)

Love, supreme power of the heart, mysterious enthusiasm
that encloses in itself all poetry, all heroism, all religion!
DELPHINE

William Hazlitt (1778–1830)

We can scarcely hate anyone that we know.
ON CRITICISM

Violent antipathies are always suspicious, and betray a
secret affinity.

TABLE-TALK

Thomas Moore (1779-1852)

No, there's nothing half so sweet in life
As love's young dream.

LOVE'S YOUNG DREAM

Lord Byron (1788-1824)

Now hatred is by far the longest pleasure;
Men love in haste, but they detest at leisure.

DON JUAN

Man's love is of man's life a thing apart,
'Tis woman's whole existence.

DON JUAN

Percy Bysshe Shelley (1792-1822)

Familiar acts are beautiful through love.

PROMETHEUS UNBOUND

All love is sweet,
Given or returned.
Common as light is love,
And its familiar voice wearies not ever.
PROMETHEUS UNBOUND

T. H. Bayly (1797-1839)

Absence makes the heart grow fonder.
ISLE OF BEAUTY

Ralph Waldo Emerson (1803-1882)

All mankind loves a lover.
LOVE

Henry Wadsworth Longfellow (1807-1882)

All your strength is in your union;
All your danger in discord
Therefore be at peace henceforward
And as brothers live together.
UNTITLED

Alfred, Lord Tennyson (1809-1892)

'Tis better to have loved and lost
Than never to have loved at all.

IN MEMORIAM

O, tell her, brief is life but love is long.

THE PRINCESS

Francis Edward Smedley (1818-1864)

All's fair in love and war.

FRANK FAIRLEGH

Leo Tolstoy (1828-1910)

All, everything that I understand, I understand only because
I love.

WAR AND PEACE

William Morris (1834-1896)

Fellowship is heaven, and lack of fellowship is hell; fellowship is life, and lack of fellowship is death; and the deeds that ye do upon the earth, it is for fellowship's sake that ye do them.

UNTITLED

W. S. Gilbert (1836-1911)

It's love that makes the world go round!

IOLANTHE

Friedrich Wilhelm Nietzsche (1844-1900)

This is the hardest of all: to close the open hand out of love, and to keep modest as a giver.

THUS SPAKE ZARATHUSTRA

Ellen Key (1849-1926)

Love is moral even without legal marriage, but marriage is immoral without love.

THE MORALITY OF WOMAN

René Bazin (1853-1932)

There is no need to go searching for a remedy for the evils of the time. The remedy already exists—it is the gift of one's self to those who have fallen so low that even hope fails them. Open wide your heart.

REDEMPTION

Arthur Rimbaud (1854-1891)

Dress up, dance, laugh. I will never be able to throw Love out of the window.

LES ILLUMINATIONS

George Bernard Shaw (1856-1950)

Hate is the coward's revenge for being humiliated.

MAJOR BARBARA

Jerome K. Jerome (1859-1927)

Love is like the measles; we all have to go through it.

"ON BEING IN LOVE," IN *IDLE THOUGHTS OF AN IDLE FELLOW*

Rabindranath Tagore (1861-1941)

It is said in one of the Upanishads: It is not that thou loves—
thy son because thou desirest him, but thou lovest thy son
because thou desirest thine own soul. The meaning of this
is, that whomsoever we love, in him we find our own soul
in the highest sense. The final truth of our existence lies in
this. *Paramatma*, the supreme soul, is in me, as well as in my
son, and my joy in my son is the realization of this truth. It
has become quite a commonplace fact, yet it is wonderful to
think upon, that the joys and sorrows of our loved ones are
joys and sorrows to us—nay, they are more. Why so? Because
in them we have grown larger, in them we have touched that
great truth which comprehends the whole universe.

SOUL CONSCIOUSNESS

Rudyard Kipling (1865-1936)

A fool there was and he made his prayer (Even as you and I!)
To a rag and a bone and a hank of hair
(We called her the woman who did not care)
But the fool he called her his lady fair—
Even as you and I.

THE VAMPIRE

William Butler Yeats (1865-1939)

A pity beyond all telling
Is hid in the heart of love.

THE PITY OF LOVE

Willa Cather (1873-1947)

I tell you there is such a thing as creative hate.

THE SONG OF THE LARK

W. Somerset Maugham (1874-1965)

When you have loved as she has loved, you grow old beautifully.

THE CIRCLE

Thomas Mann (1875-1955)

It is love, not reason, that is stronger than death.

THE MAGIC MOUNTAIN

Hazrat Inayat Khan (1882-1927)

Many religions and philosophies have considered the sex-relationship to be most sacred, since it is thus that the spirit manifests itself. And for the same reason the sex-relationship may become most sinful, if this purpose of the spirit is lost to view. For to disregard this purpose of the spirit is a defiance of the law of the whole mechanism, which inevitably drags the structure to ruins.

THE SUFI MESSAGE OF HAZRAT INAYAT KHAN: THE ART OF PERSONALITY

Love, like a flame, cannot fail to give out light.

THE SUFI MESSAGE OF HAZRAT INAYAT KHAN: THE ART OF PERSONALITY

So far as human understanding can probe, it can discover nothing of greater purpose and value to the world than passion. Under that covering is hidden the hand of the creator.

THE SUFI MESSAGE OF HAZRAT INAYAT KHAN: THE ART OF PERSONALITY

James Joyce (1882-1941)

Her image had passed into his soul for ever and no word had broken the holy silence of his ecstasy.

PORTRAIT OF THE ARTIST AS A YOUNG MAN

Coco Chanel (1883-1971)

Great loves, too, must be endured.

QUOTED IN *COCO CHANEL, HER LIFE, HER SECRETS*, MARCEL HAEDRICH

D. H. Lawrence (1885-1930)

Some men want the path of love to run pleasantly between allotment-gardens stocked with cabbages and potatoes and an occasional sweet-william; some men want rose-avenues

and trickling streams, and so scratch themselves and get gnat-
bitten; some want to scale unheard-of heights, roped to some
extraordinary female of their fancy. *Chacun à son gout.*
PHOENIX II

Gabriela Mistral (1889-1957)

I dream of a vase of humble and simple clay,
to keep your ashes near my watchful eyes;
and for you my cheek will be the wall of the vase
and my soul and your soul will be satisfied.
I will not sift them into a vase of burning gold,
not into a pagan urn that mimics carnal lines;
I want only a vase of simple clay to hold
you humbly like a fold in this skirt of mine.
One of these afternoons I'll gather clay
by the river, and I'll shape it with trembling hand.
Women, bearing sheaves, will pass my way,
not guessing I fashion a bed for a husband.
The fistful of dust, I hold in my hands,
will noiseless pour, like a thread of tears.

I will seal this vase with an infinite kiss,

and I'll cover you only with my endless gaze!

"THE VASE," IN LOVE POEMS: FROM SPAIN AND
SPANISH AMERICA

Dorothy Parker (1893-1967)

Oh, life is a glorious cycle of song,

A medley of extemporanea;

And love is a thing that can never go wrong,

And I am Marie of Roumania.

COMMENT

By the time you swear you're his Shivering and sighing,

And he vows his passion is Infinite, undying—

Lady make a note of this: One of you is lying.

UNFORTUNATE COINCIDENCE

Meher Baba (1894-1969)

The Beloved is devoted to its lovers for how else can it be
Belovedness? Each and every Lover is the beloved; each
and every Beloved is the Lover. The Absolute Unity, which
is the Absolute Beauty and Absolute Love, loves its Beloved
so intensely it leaves not a trace of themselves. For in reality
there is only the Beloved, only loving.

*GOD SPEAKS—THE THEME OF CREATION
AND ITS PURPOSE*

J. Krishnamurti (1895-1986)

Love is vulnerable, pliable, receptive; it is the highest form
of sensitivity, and identification makes for insensitivity.
Identification and love do not go together, for the one
destroys the other.

*COMMENTARIES ON LIVING—FROM THE NOTEBOOKS
OF J. KRISHNAMURTI*

Love admits no division. Either you love, or do not love....

*COMMENTARIES ON LIVING—FROM THE NOTEBOOKS
OF J. KRISHNAMURTI*

Wei Wu Wei (1895-1986)

Unless you can hate you cannot possibly love.
And vice versa.

OPEN SECRET

Joseph Campbell (1904-1987)

In so far as love expresses itself, it is not expressing itself in
terms of socially approved manners of life. That's why it is all
so secret. Love has nothing to do with social order. It is a higher
spiritual experience than that of socially organized marriage.

Pablo Neruda (1904-1973)

Your breast is enough for my heart,
and my wings for your freedom.
What was sleeping above your soul will rise
out of your mouth to heaven.
In you is the illusion of each day.
You arrive like the dew to the cupped flowers.
You undermine the horizon with your absence.
Eternally in flight like the wave.

TWENTY LOVE POEMS AND A SONG OF DESPAIR

Albert Camus (1913-1960)

When one has once had the good luck to love intensely, life is spent in trying to recapture that ardor and that illumination.
RETURN TO TIPASA

Osho (1931-1990)

When I say "Love yourself," this is for those who have never gone inside, because they can always…they are bound to understand only a language of duality. Love yourself—that means you are dividing yourself into two, the lover and the loved. You may not have thought about it, but if you go inside you will not love yourself, you will be love.
DISCOURSES

If I love someone, immediately my mind will start working on how to marry them, because marriage fixes things. Love is a flux, love cannot be predicted. No one knows where it will lead, or whether it will lead anywhere.
DISCOURSES

Lawrence Durrell (1912-1990)

It is not love that is blind, but jealousy.

JUSTINE

Gabriel García Marquez (Contemporary)

The only regret I will have in dying is if it is not for love.

LOVE IN THE TIME OF CHOLERA

Javad Nurbakhsh (1926-2008)

I thought of You so often that I completely became You. Little by little You drew near, and slowly but slowly I passed away.

IN THE TAVERN OF RUIN

Erich Segal (Contemporary)

Love means never having to say you're sorry.

LOVE STORY

Jane Wyman (1917-2007)

The opportunity to practice brotherhood presents itself every time you meet a human being.

SPOKEN

MAN AND WOMANKIND

Protagoras (c. 481–411 BCE)
Man is the measure of all things.
CONCERNING THE GODS

The Dhammapada (3rd Century BCE)
Let man be free from pleasure and let man be free from pain;
for not to have pleasure is sorrow and to have pain is also sorrow.
From pleasure arises sorrow and from pleasure arises fear. If a
man is free from pleasure, he is free from fear and sorrow.

There never was, there never will be, nor is there now,
a man whom men always blame, or a man whom they
always praise.

Cicero (106-43 BCE)

No man was ever great without divine inspiration.

DE NATURA DEORUM

Virgil (70-19 BCE)

We are not all capable of everything.

ECLOGUES

Plotinus (203-262)

Man as he now is has ceased to be the All. When he ceases to be a separate individual, he raises himself again and penetrates the whole world.

ENNEADS

Mahmud Shabistari (1250-1320)

Nonbeing is a mirror, the world an image, and man is the eye of the image in which the person is hidden. You are the eye of the image and the light of the eye. Who has ever seen the eye through which all things are seen? The world has become a man and man a world. There is no clearer explanation than this. When you look well into the root of the matter He is at once seen, both seeing eye and thing seen.

THE GARDEN OF MYSTERY

Marie Anne du Deffand (1697-1780)

I do not know why Diogenes [a Greek philosopher] went looking for a man: Nothing could happen to him worse than finding one.

CORRESPONDANCE INÉDITE

Chief Seattle (1786-1866)

This we know. The Earth does not belong to man; man belongs to the Earth. This we know. All things are connected like blood which unites one family. All things are connected. Whatever befalls the Earth befalls the sons of the Earth. Man did not weave the web of life; he is merely a strand in it. Whatever he does to the web, he does to himself.

HIS ADDRESS, 1853

Fyodor Dostoevsky (1821-1881)

Man is a creature that can get used to anything, and I think
that is the best definition of him.

THE HOUSE OF THE DEAD

It sometimes happened that you might be familiar with a
man for several years thinking he was a wild animal, and
you would regard him with contempt. And then suddenly a
moment would arrive when some uncontrollable impulse
would lay his soul bare, and you would behold in it such
riches, such sensitivity and warmth, such a vivid awareness
of its own suffering and the suffering of others, that the
scales would fall from your eyes and at first you would hardly
be able to believe what you had seen and heard. The reverse
also happens.

THE HOUSE OF THE DEAD

Robert Louis Stevenson (1850-1894)

Every man is his own doctor of divinity, in the last resort.

AN INLAND VOYAGE, NOYON

Havelock Ellis (1859-1939)

Civilized men arrive in the Pacific, armed with alcohol, syphilis, trousers, and the Bible.

THE DANCE OF LIFE

Margot Asquith (1864-1945)

The spirit of man is an inward flame, a lamp the world blows upon but never puts out.

AUTOBIOGRAPHY

Maria Montessori (1870-1952)

Humanity is still far from that stage of maturity needed for the realization of its aspirations, for the construction, that is, of a harmonious and peaceful society and the elimination of wars. Men are not yet ready to shape their own destinies, to control and direct world events, of which—instead—they become the victims.

THE ABSORBENT MIND

The Mother (1878-1973)

I am sure the movement has begun…. How long it will take
to arrive at a concrete, visible, and organized reality I don't
know. Something has begun. It seems it's going to be the
onrush of the new species, the new creation, or at any rate
a new creation. A reorganization of the earth and a new
creation…but even today, the overwhelming majority of
people and intellectuals are perfectly content with taking care
of themselves and their little rounds of progress. They don't
even want anything else! Which means that the advent of
the next being may well go unnoticed, or be misunderstood
It's hard to tell since there is no precedent to compare it with;
but more than likely, if one of the great apes ever ran into
the first man, it must simply have felt that that being was
a little… strange. That's all. Men are used to thinking that
anything higher than they has to be…divine beings—that
is, without a body—who appear in a burst of light. In other
words, all the gods as they are conceived—but it isn't like that
at all. It is almost as if a new mind is being formed And the
body is learning its lesson—all bodies, all bodies.

SATPREM, THE MIND OF THE CELL

Nikos Kazantzakis (1885–1957)

Every one follows his own bent. Man is like a tree. You've never quarreled with a fig tree because it doesn't bear cherries, have you?

ZORBA THE GREEK

Every man has his folly, but the greatest folly of all…is not to have one.

ZORBA THE GREEK

J. Krishnamurti (1895–1986)

Inequality is a fact, and no revolution can do away with it.

COMMENTARIES ON LIVING–FROM THE NOTEBOOKS OF J. KRISHNAMURTI

Alan Watts (1915–1973)

The Highest to which man can attain is wonder; and if the prime phenomenon makes him wonder, let him be content; nothing higher can it give him, and nothing further should he seek for behind it; here is the limit.

THE BOOK

Osho (1931-1990)

Remove God and put man in his place, and you will have a totally different world. The suffering is absolutely unwanted. The anguish is our stupidity. Man can live a tremendously rich, blissful, ecstatic life. But the first thing is, he has to accept his responsibility.

DISCOURSES

Man is upset when he cannot show that he carries a big load on his back, so another interesting feature emerges: he generally boasts a bigger load than he actually has.

DISCOURSES

Carlos Castaneda (1925-1998)

I care so much for my fellow man…that I don't do anything for him. I wouldn't know what to do. And I would always have the nagging sense that I was imposing my will on him with my gifts.

THE FIRE WITHIN

Da Free John (1939-2008)

Man is only a brief design in the numberless evolutionary stages of the World. And the individual human being is only a moment, a specimen, a partial realization of Man. The individual is not made for his own sake, but to be sacrificed toward Man—so that Man may fulfill his evolutionary destiny. And Man is not made for his own sake, but to be sacrificed toward the ultimate evolutionary process of the World. And the World is not made for its own sake, but to be sacrificed to the unqualified and Eternal Divine.

THE ENLIGHTENMENT OF THE WHOLE BODY

Adrien-Emmanuel Roquette (1813-1887)

Man is the medium between spirit and matter; he is between the visible and the invisible world. He sums them up in his person, as in a universal center.

Morris West (1916-1999)

Man is the only significant link between the physical order
and the spiritual one. Without man the universe is a howling
wasteland contemplated by an unseen Deity.

THE SHOES OF THE FISHERMAN

MEDITATION

The Upanishads (c. 900-600 BCE)

Where the channels are brought together
Like the spokes in the hub of a wheel—
Therein he moves about,
Becoming manifold.
Om!—Thus meditate upon the Soul.
Success to you in crossing to the farther shore beyond
    darkness!
He who is all-knowing, all wise,
Whose is this greatness on the earth—
He is in the divine Brahma city
And in the heaven established! The Soul!
Consisting of mind, leader of the life-breaths and of the body,
He is established on food, controlling the heart.

By this knowledge the wise perceive
The blissful Immortal that gleams forth.

THE SECOND KHANDA

The Bhagavad Gita (c. 500 BCE)

He who is every content and meditative, self-subjugated and possessed with firm conviction, with mind and heart dedicated to Me, he who is thus consecrated to Me is dear to Me.

Saraha (1st or 2nd Century)

This world of appearance has from its radiant beginning
Never come to be; unpatterned it has discarded patterning.
As such it is continuous and unique meditation;
It is non meditation, stainless contemplation, and nonmind.

THE ROYAL SONG OF SARAHA

Milarepa (1040-1123)

If there is joy in meditation upon the sun and moon,
the planets and fixed stars are the magic creation of the sun
and moon;

make thyself like unto the sun and moon themselves.
If there is joy in meditation upon the mountain,
the fruit-trees are the magic creation of the mountain;
make thy self like the mountain itself.

If there is joy in meditation upon thine own mind,
distinctive thought is the magic creation of the mind;
make thyself like unto the mind itself.

THE MESSAGE OF MILAREPA

Isaac of Acco (13th–14th Century)

A sage once came to one of the meditators and asked that he be accepted into their society. The other replied, "My son, blessed are you to God. Your intentions are good. But tell me, have you attained stoicism?" The sage said, "Master, explain your words." The meditator said, "If one man is praising you and another is insulting you, are the two equal in your eyes or not?" He replied, "No, my master, I have pleasure from those who praise me, and pain from those who degrade me. But I do not take revenge or bear a grudge." The other said, "Go in peace my son. You have not attained stoicism. You have not reached a level where your soul does not feel the praise of one who honors you, nor the degradation of one who insults you. You are not prepared for your thoughts to bound on high, that you should come and meditate. Go and increase the humbleness of your heart, and learn to treat everything equally until you have become stoic. Only then will you be able to meditate."

THE LIGHT OF THE EYES

Michel de Montaigne (1533–1592)

Meditation is a rich and powerful method of study for anyone who knows how to examine his mind, and to employ it vigorously. I would rather shape my soul than furnish it. There is no exercise that is either feebler or more strenuous, according to the nature of the mind concerned, than that of conversing with one's own thoughts. The greatest men make it their vocation, "those for whom to live is to think" [a quotation from the philosopher Cicero]. Moreover, nature has favored it with this privilege, that there is nothing we can do for so long at a time, nor any action to which we can apply ourselves more frequently and easily. It is the occupation of the gods, says Aristotle, the source from which comes their beatitude and ours.

ESSAYS

Shivapuri Baba (1826-1963)

Meditation is profound thinking. It makes our health better, gives extremely helpful ideas, and is quite essential for our spiritual progress. Meditation is a mad man's business.

QUOTED IN *LONG PILGRIMAGE*, J. G. BENNETT

Only if our life is exactly regulated, will we have the time and energy required for meditation. Right meditation cannot be based upon a disordered life.

QUOTED IN *LONG PILGRIMAGE*, J. G. BENNETT

Yogaswami (1872-1964)

When you have entirely surrendered, everything you do will be meditation.

POSITIVE THOUGHTS FOR DAILY MEDITATION

Meditate in the morning and evening and at night before you go to bed. Sit quietly for about two minutes. You will find everything in your life falling into place and your prayers answered.

POSITIVE THOUGHTS FOR DAILY MEDITATION

Pierre Teilhard de Chardin (1881-1955)

Lord, lock me up in the deepest depths of your heart; and then, holding me there, burn me, purify me, set me on fire, sublimate me, till I become utterly what you would have me be, through the utter annihilation of my ego.

THE MASS ON THE WORLD

J. Krishnamurti (1895-1986)

Meditation is not a means to an end. It is both the means and the end.

THE SECOND PENGUIN KRISHNAMURTI READER

Any form of conscious meditation is not the real thing: It can never be. Deliberate attempt to meditate is not meditation. It must happen; it cannot be invited. Meditation is not the play of the mind nor of desire and pleasure. All attempt to meditate is the very denial of it. Only be aware of what you are thinking and doing and nothing else. The seeing, the hearing, is the doing, without reward and punishment.

THE SECOND PENGUIN KRISHNAMURTI READER

Meditation is danger for it destroys everything, nothing whatsoever is left, not even a whisper of desire, and in this vast, unfathomable emptiness there is creation and love.

THE SECOND PENGUIN KRISHNAMURTI READER

The flower is the form, the scent, the color, and the beauty that is the whole of it. Tear it to pieces actually or verbally, then there is not flower, only the remembrance of what it was, which is never the flower. Meditation is the whole flower in its beauty, withering and living.

THE SECOND PENGUIN KRISHNAMURTI READER

Meditation is the freeing of energy in abundance; and control, discipline, and suppression spoil the purity of that energy.

THE SECOND PENGUIN KRISHNAMURTI READER

Wei Wu Wei (1895-1986)

The practice of meditation is represented by the three famous monkeys, who cover their eyes, ears, and mouths so as to avoid the...world. The practice of non-meditation is ceasing to be the seer, hearer, or speaker while eyes, ears, and mouths are fulfilling their function in daily life.

OPEN SECRET

Osho (1931-1990)

Meditation is pure space, undisturbed by knowledge

DISCOURSES

Meditation is nothing but coming back home, just to have a little rest inside. It is not the chanting of a mantra, it is not even a prayer, it is just coming back home and having a little rest.

DISCOURSES

Sogyal Rinpoche (Contemporary)

Fortunately we live in a time when all over the world many people are becoming familiar with meditation. It is being increasingly accepted as a practice that cuts through and soars above cultural and religious barriers, and enables those who pursue it to establish a direct contact with the truth of their being. It is a practice that at once transcends the dogma of religions and is the essence of religions.

THE TIBETAN BOOK OF LIVING AND DYING

Eliezer Shore (Contemporary)

The contemplative is to the community what the soul is to the body.

PARABOLA

MIND

The Upanishads (c. 900-600 BCE)

Moved by whom does thinking attain its object?
Who directs the function of vital breathing?
Moved by whom do people engage in speaking?
Say what force directs both the sight and hearing,
He, the hearing's Hearer, the thinking's Thinker,
speaking's Speaker, even the breathing's Breather.
Eye of eye. The wise by renouncing find Him;
parting from this World they become immortal.

KENA UPANISHAD

The Bhagavad Gita (c. 500 BCE)

The mind is indeed restless, Arjuna: it is indeed hard to train.
But by constant practice and by freedom from passions the
mind in truth can be trained.

When the mind is not in harmony, this divine communion
is hard to attain; but the man whose mind is in harmony
attains it, if he knows and if he strives.

The Dhammapada (3rd Century BCE)

What we are today comes from our thoughts of yesterday,
and our present thoughts build our life of tomorrow: Our life
is the creation of our mind.

If a man speaks or acts with an impure mind, suffering
follows him as the wheel of the cart follows the beast that
draws the cart.

If a man speaks or acts with a pure mind, joy follows him
as his own shadow.

THE PATH TO PERFECTION

Make haste and do what is good; keep your mind away from evil. If a man is slow in doing good, his mind finds pleasure in evil.

THE PATH OF PERFECTION

Virgil (70-19 BCE)
Practice and thought might gradually forge many an art.

GEORGES I

Happy the man who could search out the causes of things.

GEORGIES I

The Gospel of Mary (c. 100)
"I," she said, "I saw the Lord in a vision and I said to him, 'Lord, I saw you today in a vision.' He answered and said to me, 'Blessed are you, since you did not waver at the sight of me. For where the mind is, there is your countenance.' I said to him, 'Lord, the mind which sees the vision, does it see it through the soul or though the spirit?' The Savior answered and said, 'It sees neither through the soul nor through the

spirit, but the mind, which is between the two, which sees the vision.'"

ATTRIBUTED TO MARY MAGDALENE, FROM
*GNOSTICISM: A SOURCEBOOK OF HERETICAL
WRITINGS*, ROBERT GRANT

Saint Augustine (354-430)

For I remember the kind of man I was, O Lord, and it is a sweet task to confess how you tamed me by pricking my heart with your goad; how you bridged every valley, leveled every mountain and hill of my thoughts; how you cut straight through their windings, paved their rough paths.
CONFESSIONS.

Lankavatara Sutra (4th Century CE)

It is like an image reflected in a mirror, it is seen but it is not real; the one Mind is seen as a duality by the ignorant when it is reflected in the mirror constructed by our memory…the existence of the entire universe is due to memory that has been accumulated since the beginningless past but wrongly interpreted.

Shankara (788-820)

The Self never undergoes change; the intellect never possesses consciousness. But when one sees all this world, he is deluded into thinking, "I am the seer, I am the knower." Mistaking one's Self for the individual entity, like the rope mistaken for the snake, one is overcome with fear. If one knows oneself not as the individual but as the supreme Self, one becomes free from fear.

MEDITATIONS

Milarepa (1040-1123)

I have already fully realized that all beings and all phenomena are of one's own mind. The mind itself is a transparency of Voidness. What, therefore, is the use of all this, and how foolish I am to try to dispel these manifestations physically.

THE HUNDRED THOUSAND SONGS OF MILAREPA

Saint Thomas Aquinas (1224/5-1274)

Reason in man is rather like God in the world.

OPUSCULE II, DE REGNO

Mira Bai (1498-1546)

What is beyond the mind,
has no boundary,
In it our senses end.

DEVOTIONAL POEMS

Michel de Montaigne (1533-1592)

I imagine virtue to be both something else and something nobler than the propensity toward goodness that is born in us. The well-disposed and naturally well-controlled mind follows the same course as the virtuous, and presents the same appearance in its actions. But virtue sounds like some greater and more active thing than merely to let oneself be led by a happy disposition quietly and peaceably along the path of reason. One who out of natural mildness and good nature overlooks injuries received performs a very fine and praiseworthy action; but another who, though provoked and stung to anger by an insult, takes up the weapons of reason against his furious desire for revenge, and

after hard battle finally masters it, is undoubtedly doing a great
deal more. The first man is behaving well, the second virtuously;
the first action might be called goodness, the second virtue.
For the word virtue, I think, presupposes difficulty and struggle,
and something that cannot be practiced without an adversary.
This is perhaps why we call God good, mighty, liberal, and just,
but do not call Him virtuous; His workings are all natural
and effortless.

ESSAYS

William Shakespeare (1564-1616)

There is nothing either good or bad but thinking makes it so.

HAMLET, II, 2, 253

John Donne (1572-1631)

Reason is our soul's left hand, Faith her right,
By these we reach divinity.

TO THE COUNTESS OF BEDFORD

Elizabeth Clinton (c. 1574–1630)

Whatsoever things are true, whatsoever things are honest…
whatsoever things are just, whatsoever things are pure,
whatsoever things are of good report…think on these things;
these things do, and the God of peace shall be with you.

LETTERS

Sarmad (17th Century)

O my friend! Remain in solitude with a passion to meet
    the Lord;
Rid thyself of all grief and be happy.
Be not like the whirlwind; be not baffled or perplexed.
Centre thy mind on one point, and be free from all thought.

RUBAIYATS OF SARMAD 226

Mr. Tut-Tut (c. 17th Century)

The proud spirit, the chivalric spirit, and the beautiful spirit
suffuse fragrance even when their bones are dead; words
of cool detachment, witty words, and words of charm carry
weight though their volume be small.

ONE HUNDRED PROVERBS

Walt Whitman (1819-1892)

Do I contradict myself? Very well then I contradict myself;
(I am large—I contain multitudes.)

"SONG OF MYSELF," IN *LEAVES OF GRASS*

Shivapuri Baba (1826-1963)

One should have no liking, one should have no disliking.
Reason must prevail.

LECTURES

Suppose you like me: You will give me everything. Suppose
you hate me: you will give me nothing. This is under the
influence of like and disliking. Under the influence of reason,
what will you do? You will see if I deserve or not. Suppose I
am your enemy; still, if I deserve, you will give me. Suppose
I am your friend; if I do not deserve, you will not give me.
This is the direction of reason. This reason must always
prevail. Liking and disliking must perish.

QUOTED IN *LONG PILGRIMAGE*, J. G. BENNETT

Sigmund Freud (1856-1939)

The voice of the intellect is a soft one, but it does not rest until it has gained a hearing. Ultimately, after endless repeated rebuffs, it succeeds. This is one of the few points in which one may be optimistic about the future of mankind but in itself it signifies not a little.

FUTURE OF AN ILLUSION

Bernard Berenson (1865-1959)

Consistency requires you to be as ignorant today as you were a year ago.

NOTEBOOK, 1892

Yogaswami (1872-1964)

One method is to stop all thought. Another method is to remain simply as a witness, allowing thoughts to come and go. As one becomes more and more mature in this practice, thoughts will begin to come from the inner silence. Be very attentive to these thoughts.

POSITIVE THOUGHTS FOR DAILY MEDITATION

If you try to stop the mind, it will only become more active.
It is not necessary to stop it. You must ask it where it is going.
POSITIVE THOUGHTS FOR DAILY MEDITATION

If the chimney if full of smoke, how can the light be seen?
If the mind is full of dirt, how can the soul shine?
POSITIVE THOUGHTS FOR DAILY MEDITATION

G. K. Chesterton (1874–1936)

It is not natural to see man as a natural product. It is not
common sense to call man a common object of the country or
the seashore. It is not seeing straight to see him as an animal.
It is not sane…. If we imagine that an inhuman or impersonal
intelligence could have felt from the first the general nature
of the nonhuman world sufficiently to see that things would
evolve in whatever way they did evolve, there would have been
nothing whatever in all that natural world to prepare such a
mind for such an unnatural novelty…. Suppose that one bird
out of a thousand birds began to do one of the thousand things
that man had already done even in the morning of the world;

and we can be quite certain that the onlooker would not regard such a bird as a mere evolutionary variety of the other birds; he would regard it as a very fearful wild-fowl indeed....That bird would tell the augurs, not of something that would happen, but of something that had happened. That something would be the appearance of a mind with a new dimension of depth; a mind like that of man. If there be no God, no other mind could conceivably have foreseen it.

THE EVERLASTING MAN

Ramana Maharshi (1879-1950)

Have you not heard of the saying of Vivekananda, that if one but thinks a noble, selfless thought even in a cave, it sets up vibrations throughout the world and does what has to be done—what can be done?

DISCOURSE

D. H. Lawrence (1885-1930)

Emotions by themselves become just a nuisance. The mind by itself becomes just a sterile thing, making everything sterile. So what's to be done?

You've got to marry the pair of them. Apart, they are no good. The emotions that have not the approval and inspiration of the mind are just hysterics. The mind without the approval and inspiration of the emotions is just a dry stick, a dead tree, no good for anything unless to make a rod to beat and bully somebody with.

PHOENIX II

Man is a thought-adventurer.

Which isn't the same as saying that man has intellect…. Real thought is an experience. It begins as a change in the blood, a slow convulsion and revolution in the body itself. It ends as a new piece of awareness, a new reality in mental consciousness.

On this account, thought is an adventure, and not a practice. In order to think, man must risk himself. He must risk himself doubly. First, he must go forth and meet life in the body. Then he must face the result in his mind.

PHOENIX II

Erwin Schrödinger (1887-1961)

Mind is always now. There is really no before and after for mind. There is only a now that includes memories and expectations.

MY LIFE

Ludwig Wittgenstein (1889-1951)

Suppose someone were a believer and said: "I believe in a Last Judgment," and I said: "Well, I'm not so sure. Possibly." You would say that there is an enormous gulf between us. If he said: "There is a German airplane overhead," and I said: "Possibly. I'm not so sure," you'd say we were fairly near.

LECTURES ON RELIGIOUS BELIEF

J. Krishnamurti (1895-1986)

Freedom is emptying the mind of experience. When the brain ceases to nourish itself through experience, then its activity is not self-centered. It then has its nourishment that makes the mind religious.

The mind is the true ruler, the true helper, the true guide; but the mind is also the destroyer, if misused. The mind, when properly used, should be the guiding force for the majority of us. Though we may not be intellectual giants, we have ordinary intelligence, ordinary perception, and the power to balance things. When you use the mind in this manner, you have a tremendous helper, a great power to build, to create.

THE POOL OF WISDOM

The very activity of the mind is a barrier to its own understanding.

COMMENTARIES ON LIVING – FROM THE NOTEBOOKS OF J. KRISHNAMURTI

Albert Camus (1913-1960)

All great deeds and all great thoughts have ridiculous beginnings. Great works are often born on a street-corner or in a restaurant's revolving door.

THE MYTH OF SISYPHUS

Osho (1931–1990)

The Indian system of reasoning is not like investigating truth with the help of a lamp. It is like investigating the dark night in the dazzling brilliance of a lightning flash, where everything becomes visible simultaneously. Not that something—a part—is seen now, sometime later another part, later again something more, and so on; no the Indian way is not like that. In the Indian system of investigation, the revelation of truth takes place all at once; everything is discovered at one and the same time.

DISCOURSES

Ideas create stupidity because the more the ideas are there, the more the mind is burdened. And how can a burdened mind know? The more ideas are there, the more it becomes just like dust which has gathered on a mirror. How can a mirror mirror? How can the mirror reflect? Your intelligence is just covered by opinions, the dust, and everyone who is opinionated is bound to be stupid and dull.

DISCOURSES

Roberto Assagioli (Contemporary)

We think that there is such a thing as the "unconscious will" of the higher Self which tends always to bring the personality in line with the overall purpose of the spiritual Self.

PSYCHOSYNTHESIS: A MANUAL OF PRINCIPLES AND TECHNIQUES

U. G. Krishnamurti (Contemporary)

Every time a thought is born, you are born. When the thought is gone, you are gone. But the "you" does not let the thought go, and what gives continuity to this "you" is thinking. Actually there's no permanent entity in you, no totality of all your thoughts and experiences. You think that there is "somebody" who is feeling your feelings—that's the illusion. I can say it is an illusion but it is not an illusion to you.

THE MYSTIQUE OF ENLIGHTENMENT—THE UNRATIONAL IDEAS OF A MAN CALLED U. G.

Where are the thoughts located? They are not in the brain. Thoughts are not manufactured by the brain. It is, rather, that the brain is like an antenna, picking up thoughts on a common wavelength, a common thought-sphere.

MIND IS A MYTH—DISQUIETING CONVERSATIONS WITH A MAN CALLED U. G.

Emerson Pugh (Contemporary)

If the human brain were so simple that we could understand it, we would be so simple that we wouldn't.

UNTITLED

Ramtha (Contemporary)

All things are created by taking that which has no speed—thought—and expanding it into that which does—light—and then slowing the light down until you create this and that and all that is around you.

RAMTHA: AN INTRODUCTION, S. L. WEINBERG

Arthur Waley (Contemporary)

Thought grows out of environment.

TRANSLATORS INTRODUCTION TO *THE ANALECTS OF CONFUCIUS*

MYSTICISM

Lao Tzu (c. 6th Century BCE)

The Way is like an empty vessel that yet may be drawn from.

TAO TE CHING

The Way [Tao] that can be told is not the eternal way.

TAO TE CHING

Shankara (788-820)

The knower of the Atman [pure consciousness] does not identify himself with his body. He rests within it, as if within a carriage. If people provide him with comforts and luxuries, he enjoys them and plays with them like a child. He bears no outward mark of a holy man. He remains quite unattached to the things of this world.

He may wear costly clothing, or none. He may be dressed in deer or tiger skin or clothed in pure knowledge. He may seem like a madman, or like a child, or sometimes like an unclean spirit. Thus, he wanders the earth.

The man of contemplation walks alone. He lives desireless amidst the objects of desire. The Atman is his eternal satisfaction. He sees the Atman present in all things.

Sometimes he appears to be a fool, sometimes a wise man. Sometimes he seems splendid as a king, sometimes feeble-minded. Sometimes he is calm and silent. Sometimes he draws men to him, as a python attracts its prey. Sometimes people honor him greatly, sometimes they insult him. Sometimes they ignore him. That is how the illumined soul lives, always absorbed in the highest bliss.

CREST-JEWEL OF DISCRIMINATION

Saint John of the Cross (1542–1591)

The dark night of the soul through which the soul passes on its way to the Divine Light.

THE ASCENT OF MOUNT CARMEL

Benjamin Whichcote (1609-1683)

The more mysterious, the more imperfect: That which is mystically spoken is but half spoken.

MORAL AND RELIGIOUS APHORISMS

André Gide (1869-1951)

Without mysticism man can achieve nothing great.

THE COUNTERFEITERS

Bertrand Russell (1872-1970)

Mysticism is, in essence, little more than a certain intensity and depth of feeling in regard to what is believed about the universe.

MYSTICISM AND LOGIC

Evelyn Underhill (1875-1941)

Mysticism is the art of union with Reality. The mystic is a person who has attained that union in greater or less degree; or who aims at and believes in such attainment.

PRACTICAL MYSTICISM

Albert Einstein (1879-1955)

The most beautiful thing we can experience is the mysterious.
It is the source of all true art and science.

WHAT I BELIEVE

Mikhail Naimy (1889-1988)

To pierce the veils you need an eye other than that shaded
with lash and lid and brow.

To break the seals you need a lip other than the familiar
piece of flesh below the nose.

First see the eye itself aright, if you would see the other
things aright. Not with the eye, but through it must you look
that you may see all things beyond it.

THE BOOK OF MIRDAD–A LIGHTHOUSE AND A HAVEN

Alan Watts (1915-1973)

Now if we examine the records of mystical experience…we
shall find that time and time again, it is connected with
"spiritual poverty"—that is to say with giving up the ownership
of everything, including oneself or one's consciousness. It

is the total abandonment of proprietorship on the external
world of nature and the internal world of the human
organism…. When it thus becomes clear that I own nothing,
not even what I have called myself, it is as if, to use St. Paul's
words, I had nothing but possessed all things.

THIS IS IT: AND OTHER ESSAYS ON ZEN AND
SPIRITUAL EXPERIENCE

R. D. Laing (1927–1989)

Mystics and schizophrenics find themselves in the same
ocean, but the mystics swim whereas the schizophrenics
drown.

THE POLITICS OF EXPERIENCE AND THE BIRD
OF PARADISE

Roberto Assagioli (1888–1974)

The true nature of mysticism cannot be considered as some
investigators have maintained, to be merely a product or
by-product of sex. On the one hand, one finds many people
whose normal sexual life is inhibited yet who show no trace

of mysticism; on the other hand, there are instances of people leading a normal sexual life, raising a family, etc., and having at the same time genuine mystical experiences.

PSYCHOSYNTHESIS: A MANUAL OF PRINCIPLES AND TECHNIQUES

Da Free John (1939-2008)

The Adept…is a useful and remarkable Agency, a unique mechanism in nature, a hole in the universe through which the Transcendental Influence moves through to the world. Therefore, this remarkable Agency, when it occurs, should be used. It should be acknowledged and understood as it is. People should know how to relate to it, how to use it as a unique instrument of the Divine. Adepts appear to serve your Realization. Otherwise, as soon as someone entered into the sphere of Perfect Realization, he or she would be Translated, and that would be the end of it. Even if some Great Teaching appeared, there would never be the unique instrument of the Adept.

THE FIRE GOSPEL

NATURE

Anonymous
A fallen leaf returning to the branch? Butterfly.

Ancient Egypt (c. 1412 BCE)
Sole likeness, maker of what is,
Sole and only one, maker of what exists.
From whose eyes men issued,
From whose mouth the gods came forth,
Maker of herbs for the cattle,
And the tree of life for mankind.

"HYMN TO THE SUN-GOD" IN *SACRED BOOKS
OF THE WORLD*, A. C. BOUQUET

The Upanishads (c. 900-600 BCE)

My Son! Bees create honey by gathering the sweet juices from different flowers, and mixing all into a common juice.

And there is nothing in honey whereby the juice of a particular flower can be identified, so it is with the various creatures who merge in that Being, in deep sleep or in death. Whatever they may be, tiger, lion, wolf, boar, worm, moth, gnat, mosquito, they become aware of particular life when they are born into it or awake.

That Being is the seed; all else but His expression. He is truth. He is Self, Shwetaketu! You are That.

CHANDOGYA UPANISHAD

Lao Tzu (c. 6th Century BCE)

Nature is not human-hearted.

TAO TE CHING

Chuang Tzu (369-286 BCE)

There is an original nature in things. Things in their original nature are curved without the help of arcs, straight without lines, round without compasses, and rectangular without squares; they are joined together without glue and hold together without cords. In this manner, all things live and grow from an inner urge and none can tell how they come to do so. They all have a place in the scheme of things and none can tell how they come to have their proper place. From time immemorial this has always been so, and it may not be tampered with.

JOINED TOES

Zeno (335-263 BCE)

The goal of your life is living in agreement with nature.

DIOGENES LAËRTIUS, BOOK 3, SEC. 87

Lucretius (99-55 BCE)

Nature is free and uncontrolled by proud masters and runs the universe by herself without the aid of gods. For who—by the sacred hearts of the gods who pass their unruffled lives,

their placid aeon, in calm and peace!—who can rule the sum
total of the measureless? Who can hold in coercive hand the
strong reins of the unfathomable?

ON THE NATURE OF THINGS

Old Testament

And the wolf shall dwell with the lamb,
And the leopard shall lie down with the kid;
And the calf and the young lion and the fatling shall
    be together;
And a little child shall lead them.
And the cow shall graze with the bear;
Their young ones shall lie down together;
And the lion shall eat straw like the ox.
And the sucking child shall play at the hole of the asp,
And the weaned child shall put his hand on the adder's den.
None shall hurt nor destroy in all My holy mountain;
For the earth shall be full of the knowledge of the Lord,
As the waters cover the sea.

ISAIAH XI

Saraha (1st or 2nd Century)

Though the fragrance of a flower cannot be touched,
'Tis all pervasive and at once perceptible.
So by unpatterned being-in-itself
Recognize the round of mystic circles.

THE ROYAL SONG OF SARAHA

New Testament

And there arose a great storm of wind, and the waves beat
into the ship, so that it was now full. And he was in the
hinder part of the ship, asleep on a pillow: and they awake
him, and say unto him, Master, carest thou not that we
perish? And he arose, and rebuked the wind, and said unto
the sea, Peace, be still. And the wind ceased, and there was
a great calm. And he said unto them, Why are ye so fearful?
How is it that ye have no faith? And they feared exceedingly,
and said one to another, What manner of man is this, that
even the wind and the sea obey him?

MARK 4:37-41

Origen (185-254)

Thou art a second world in miniature, the sun and moon are within thee, and also the stars.

HEXAPLA

The Gemara (c. 500)

Honi Ha-Ma'aggel once saw on his travels an old man planting a carob tree. He asked him when he thought the tree would bear fruit. "After seventy years," was the reply.

"Does thou expect to live seventy years and eat the fruit of thy labor?"

"I did not find the world desolate when I entered it," said the old man, "and as my fathers planted for me before I was born, so do I plant for those who will come after me."

TA'ANIT, 23A, *THE TALMUD* QUOTED IN THE WORLD'S GREAT SCRIPTURES, LEWIS BROWNE

Huang Po (800-850)

Your true nature is something never lost to you even in moments of delusion, nor is it gained at the moment of Enlightenment.

THE ZEN TEACHING OF HUANG PO

Lady Sarashina (c. 1008)

Still no news of blossom time!
Has Spring not come this year,
Or did the flowers forget to bloom?

DIARIES

Saint Bernard (1091-1153)

You will find something more in woods than in books. Trees and stones will teach you that which you can never learn from masters.

EPISTLE 106

Jalal al-Din Rumi (1207-1273)

I died a mineral and became a plant.
I died a plant and rose an animal.
I died an animal and I was a man.
Why should I fear? When was I less by dying?
Yet once more I shall die as man, to soar
With the blessed angels; but even from angelhood
I must pass on. All except God perishes.
When I have sacrificed my angel soul,
I shall become that which no mind ever conceived.
O, let me not exist! for Nonexistence proclaims,
"To Him we shall return."

UNTITLED

Guru Nanak (1469-1539)

Air, water, and earth,
Of these are we made.
Air like the Guru [Nanak]'s word gives the breath of life
To the babe born to the great mother earth
Sired by the waters.

The day and night our nurses be
That watch over us in our infancy.
In their laps we play.
The world is our playground.
HYMNS OF GURU NANAK

Michel de Montaigne (1533-1592)

Every man carries in himself the complete pattern of
human nature.
ESSAYS

There is a certain consideration, and a general duty of
humanity, that binds us not only to the animals, which
have life and feeling, but even to the trees and plants. We
owe justice to men, and kindness and benevolence to all
other creatures who may be susceptible of it. There is
some intercourse between them and us, and some mutual
obligation.
ESSAYS

When I dance, I dance; when I sleep, I sleep: Yes, and when
I am walking by myself in a beautiful orchard, even if my
thoughts dwell for part of the time on distant events, I
bring them back for another part to the walk, the orchard
the charm of this solitude, and to myself. Nature has with
maternal care provided that the actions she has enjoined
on us for our need shall give us pleasure; and she uses not
only reason but appetite to attract us to them. It is wrong to
infringe her rules.

ESSAYS

Sir Francis Bacon (1561-1626)

Nature to be commanded, must be obeyed.

"APHORISM 129," IN *NOVUM ORGANUM*

Nature is often hidden; sometimes overcome, seldom
extinguished.

"OF NATURE IN MEN," IN *ESSAYS*

Mr. Tut-Tut (c. 17th Century)

Only watch how the flowers bloom, how the flowers fade;
say not this man is right, that man is wrong.

ONE HUNDRED PROVERBS

Matsuo Basho (1644-1694)

Lady butterfly
perfumes her wings
by floating
over the orchid.

HAIKU

Not a flaw there is
On the polished surface
Of the divine glass,
Chaste with flowers of snow.

HAIKU

Govind Singh (1666 or 1675–1708)

Could I transform all the islands
Into paper;
Could I turn the seven oceans
Into ink—
Of all the trees grown on earth
I then would mold
A pen—
Bidding Sarasvati
Guardian of Knowledge
To write, to write—
But Thou, O highest Lord,
By all this praise, wouldst not be raised
To greater glory.

MYSTIC LYRICS FROM THE INDIAN MIDDLE AGES

Isaac Watts (1674–1748)

Let dogs delight to bark and bite,
For God hath made them so;
Let bears and lions growl and fight,
For 'tis their nature, too.

HYMN

Kobayashi Issa (1763-1827)

With one another
Let's play; O sparrow
Who has no mother.

HAIKU

William Wordsworth (1770-1850)

One impulse from a vernal wood
May teach you more of man,
Of moral evil, and of good,
Than all the sages can.

UNTITLED

John Ruskin (1819-1900)

There is no climate, no place, and scarcely an hour, in which nature does not exhibit color which no mortal effort can imitate or approach. For all our artificial pigments are, even when seen under the same circumstances, dead and lightless beside her living color; nature exhibits her hues under an intensity of sunlight which trebles their brilliancy.

MODERN PAINTERS

Henri Bergson (1859-1941)

The emotion felt by a man in the presence of nature certainly counts for something in the origin of religions.

THE TWO SOURCES OF MORALITY AND RELIGION

Sri Aurobindo (1872-1950)

The quest of man for God, which becomes in the end the most ardent and enthralling of all his quests, begins with the first vague questioning of nature and a sense of something unseen both in himself and her.

THE LIFE DIVINE

Evelyn Underhill (1875-1941)

Nothing in all nature is so lovely and so vigorous, so perfectly at home in its environment, as a fish in the sea. Its surroundings give to it a beauty, quality, and power which is not its own. We take it out, and at once a poor, limp, dull thing, fit for nothing, is gasping away its life. So the soul sunk in God, living the life of prayer, is supported, filled, transformed in beauty, by a vitality and a power which are not its own.

THE GOLDEN SEQUENCE

The Mother (1878–1973)

The sublime state is the natural state! It's you who are
constantly in a state that is not natural, that is not normal,
that is false, a deformation.

SATPREM, THE MIND OF THE CELLS

Hazrat Inayat Khan (1882–1927)

A soul who is not close to nature is far away from what
is called spirituality. In order to be spiritual one must
communicate, and especially one must communicate with
nature; one must feel nature.

THE SUFI MESSAGE OF HAZRAT INAYAT KHAN:
THE ART OF PERSONALITY

All the good qualities which help to fulfill the purpose of life
are the natural inheritance that every soul brings to the earth;
and almost all the bad traits that mankind shows in its nature
are as a rule acquired after birth. This shows that goodness is
natural and badness unnatural.

THE SUFI MESSAGE OF HAZRAT INAYAT KHAN:
THE ART OF PERSONALITY

D. H. Lawrence (1885-1930)

Man fights for a new conception of life and God, as he fights to plant seeds in the spring: because he knows that is the only way to harvest. If after harvest there is winter again, what does it matter? It is just seasonable.

PHOENIX II

Alan Watts (1915-1973)

Human purposes are pursued within an immense circling universe which does not seem to me to have purpose, in our sense, at all. Nature is much more playful than purposeful, and the probability that it has no special goals for the future need not strike one as a defect. On the contrary, the processes of nature as we see them both in the surrounding world and in the involuntary aspects of our own organisms are much more like art than like business, politics, or religion. They are especially like the arts of music and dancing, which unfold themselves without aiming at future destinations. No one imagines that a symphony is supposed to improve in quality as it goes along, or that the whole object of playing it is to reach the finale. The point of music is discovered in every moment of playing and listening to it. It is the same, I feel, with the greater part of our lives, and if we are unduly absorbed in improving them we may forget altogether to live them.

THIS IS IT AND OTHER ESSAYS ON ZEN AND
SPIRITUAL EXPERIENCE

Osho (1931-1990)

Sitting silently,
Doing nothing,
Spring comes,
And the grass grows by itself.

DISCOURSES

Carlos Castaneda (1925-1998)

For don Juan, then, the reality of our day-to-day life consists of an endless flow of perceptual interpretations which we, the individuals who share a specific *membership*, have learned to make in common.

JOURNEY TO IXTLAN

Kenneth Tanemura (Contemporary)

A single petal
Of the cherry blossom fell:
Mountain silence.

HAIKU

Davi Kopenawa Tanomami
(Contemporary)

We don't have poor people. Every one of us can use the land, can clear a garden, can hunt, fish. An Indian, when he needs to eat, kills just one or two tapirs.

He only cuts down a few trees to make his garden. He doesn't annihilate the animals and the forest. The whites do this….

CHIEF OF A BRAZILIAN YANOMAMI TRIBE

ONƐNƐSS

The Upanishads (c. 900-600 BCE)

Know that the Self is the master,
the body is the car, 'tis plain;
Know the intellect as the driver.
and the mind of course the rein.
The senses are the horses, sure,
the objects, roads that here, there wind;
The wise him call the enjoyer.
combined with body, sense, and mind

KATHA UPANISHAD

Everything here is Brahman: He is That
From which all things originate;
That which sustains all things;
That into which all things will be dissolved
so no one should meditate in tranquillity.
CHANDOGYA UPANISHAD

Lao Tzu (c. 6th Century BCE)

Tao invariably takes no action, and yet there is nothing
   left undone.
Reversion is the action of Tao.
Weakness is the function of Tao.
All things in the world come from being.
And being comes from nonbeing.
TAO TE CHING

The Bhagavad Gita (c. 500 BCE)

Forsaking egoism, power, pride, lust, anger. and possession
freed from the notion of "mine" and tranquil; one is thus fit
to become one with the Supreme. Becoming one with the

Supreme, serene-minded, he neither grieves nor desires; alike to all beings, he attains supreme devotion unto Me.

He who is established and unshaken; he who is alike in pleasure and pain, who is the same in pleasant and unpleasant, in praise and blame, and steady, he who is alike in honor and dishonor, the same to friend and foe, giving up all selfish undertakings, he is said to have crossed beyond the qualities of Nature. And He who, crossing over these qualities, serves Me with unwavering devotion, becomes fit to attain oneness with the Supreme.

BOOK OF DAILY THOUGHTS AND PRAYERS

Chuang Tzu (369–286 BCE)

Take, for instance, a twig and a pillar or the ugly person and the great beauty and all the strange and monstrous transformation. These are all leveled together by Tao. Division is the same as creation; creation is the same as destruction.

ON LEVELING ALL THINGS

Saraha (1st or 2nd Century)

It arises as a thing and into no thing fades,
Having no essence when will it arise again?
Without end or beginning, that which links both is not found.
Stay! The gracious master speaks.
Look and listen, touch and eat,
Smell and wander, sit and stand,
Pass your time in easy talk,
Let mind go, move not from singleness.

THE ROYAL SONG OF SARAHA

Marcus Aurelius (121-180)

Being is as it were a torrent, in and out of which bodies pass,
coalescing and cooperating with the whole, as the various
parts in us so with one another.

MEDIATIONS

Jalal al-Din Rumi (1207-1273)

I have put duality away, I have seen that the two worlds are one: one I seek, one I know, one I see, one I call. He is the first, he is the last. He is the outward, he is the inward.

QUOTED FROM *THE SOUL: AN ARCHEOLOGY*,
CLAUDIA SETZER

John Donne (1572-1631)

No man is an *Island*, entire of itself; every man is a piece of *Continent*, a part of the *main*, if a *clod* be washed away by the *sea*, *Europe* is the less, as well as if a *promontory* were, as well as if a *manor* or thy *friends* or of *thine own* were; any man's *death* diminishes *me*, because I am involved in *Mankind*;

MEDITATION

Rabindranath Tagore (1861-1941)

Joy is the realization of oneness, the oneness of our soul with the world and of the world-soul with the supreme love.

QUOTED FROM *THE SOUL: AN ARCHEOLOGY*,
CLAUDIA SETZER

Erwin Schrödinger (1887–1961)

Thus you can throw yourself flat on the ground, stretched out upon Mother Earth, with the certain conviction that you are one with her and she with you. You are as firmly established, as invulnerable as she, indeed a thousand times firmer and more invulnerable. As surely as she will engulf you tomorrow, so surely will she bring you forth anew to new striving and suffering. And not merely "some day": now, today, every day she is bringing you forth, *not once* but thousands of times, just as every day she engulfs you a thousand times over. For eternally and always there is only *now*, one and the same now; the present is the only thing that no end.

MY VIEW OF THE WORLD

Alan Watts (1915–1973)

Just as the study of natural history was first an elaborate classification of the separate species and only recently involved ecology, the study of the interrelation of species, so intelligence as a whole is at first no more than a division of the world into things and events. This overstresses the independence and separateness of things, and of ourselves from them, as things among things. It is the later task of intelligence to appreciate the inseparable relationships between the things so divided, and so to rediscover the universe as distinct from a mere multiverse. In so doing it will see its own limitations, see that intelligence alone is not enough—that it cannot operate, cannot *be* intelligence, without an approach to the world though instinctual feeling with its possibility of *knowing* relationship as you know when you drink it that water is cold.

THIS IS IT: AND OTHER ESSAYS ON ZEN AND SPIRITUAL EXPERIENCE

PRAYER

Homer (c. 900 BCE)

Pray, for all men need the aid of the gods.

ODYSSEY

Aeschylus (c. 525-456 BCE)

Ask the gods nothing excessive.

THE SUPPLIANT WOMEN

The Bhagavad Gita (c. 500 BCE)

Fill thy mind with Me, be thou My devotee, worship Me and
bow down to Me; thus steadfastly uniting thy heart with Me
alone and regarding Me as thy Supreme Goal, thou shalt
come unto Me.

Hippocrates (c. 460-357 BCE)

Prayer indeed is good, but while calling on the gods, a man should himself lend a hand.

REGIMEN

Clement of Alexandria (150-211)

Prayer is conversation with God.

STROMATEIS

Hakim Sanai (12th Century)

When you sincerely enter into prayer,
you will come forth with all your prayers answered;
but a hundred prayers that lack sincerity
will leave you still the bungler that you are,
your work a failure; prayers said from habit
are like the dust that scatters in the wind.
The prayers that reach God's court are uttered by the soul;
the mimic remains a worthless, witless beggar,
who has chose the road to madness; on this path
prayer of the soul prevails, not barren mimicry.

THE WALLED GARDEN OF TRUTH

Moses ben Shem Tov (13th Century)

Happy is the portion of whoever can penetrate into the mysteries of his master and become absorbed into him, as it were. Especially does a man achieve this when he offers up his prayer to his master in intense devotion, his will then becoming as the flame, inseparable from the coal, and his mind concentrated on the unity of the higher firmaments, and finally on the absorption of them all into the most high firmament. Whilst a man's mouth and lips are moving, his heart and will must soar to the height of heights, so as to acknowledge the unity of the whole, in virtue of the mystery of mysteries in which all ideas, all wills, and all thoughts, find their goal.

ZOHAR

Mechtild von Magdeburg (c. 1207-1249)

A hungry man can do no deep study, and thus must god, through such default, lose the best prayers.

THE FLOWING LIGHT OF THE GODHEAD

Michel de Montaigne (1533-1592)

There are few men who would dare publish to the world the prayers they make to almighty God.

ESSAYS

Jonathan Swift (1667-1745)

Complaint is the largest tribute Heaven receives, and the sincerest part of our devotion.

THOUGHTS ON VARIOUS SUBJECTS

Gotthold Ephraim Lessing (1729-1781)

A single grateful thought raised to heaven is the most perfect prayer.

MINNA VON BARNHELM

Samuel Taylor Coleridge (1772-1834)

He prayeth best, who loveth best
All things both great and small;
For the dear God who loveth us,
He made and loveth all.

THE RIME OF THE ANCIENT MARINER

He prayeth well, who loveth well
Both man and bird and beast.
THE RIME OF THE ANCIENT MARINER

Victor Hugo (1802–1885)

Certain thoughts are prayers. There are moments when,
whatever be the attitude of the body, the soul is on its knees.
LES MISÉRABLES

Ralph Waldo Emerson (1803–1882)

Prayer is the contemplation of the facts of life from the
highest point of view.
SELF-RELIANCE

Alfred, Lord Tennyson (1809–1892)

Pray for my soul.
More things are wrought by prayer
Than this world dreams of.
"THE PASSING OF ARTHUR," IN *IDYLLS OF THE KING*

Ivan Turgenev (1818-1883)

Whatever a man prays for, he prays for a miracle. Every prayer reduces itself to this: "Great God, grant that twice two be not four."

PRAYER

Ambrose Bierce (1842-1914)

To ask that the rules of the universe be annulled on behalf of a single petitioner, confessedly unworthy.

THE DEVIL'S DICTIONARY

Kahlil Gibran (1883-1931)

You pray in your distress and in your need; would that you might pray also in the fullness of your joy and in your days of abundance.

THE PROPHET

SATORI

Bernard Berenson (1865-1959)

It was a morning in early summer. A silver haze shimmered and trembled over the lime trees. The air was laden with their fragrance. The temperature was like a caress. I remember—I need not recall—that I climbed up a tree and felt suddenly immersed in "Itness." I did not call it that name. I had no need for words. It and I were one.

SKETCH FOR A SELF PORTRAIT

The Mother (1878-1973)

The entire body became a single, extremely rapid and intense vibration, but motionless. I don't know how to explain it because it wasn't moving in space, and yet it was a vibration (meaning it wasn't immobile), but it was motionless in space.

It was in the body, as if each cell had a vibration and there was but a single block of vibrations.

SATPREM, THE MIND OF THE CELLS

Pierre Teilhard de Chardin (1881-1955)

Starting from the point at which a spark was first struck, a point…was built into me congenitally, the World gradually caught fire for me, burst into flames; how this happened all *during* my life, and *as a result of* my whole life, until it formed a great luminous mass, lit from within, that surrounded me.

THE HEART OF THE MATTER

Meher Baba (1894-1969)

And spontaneously there occurred a sort of eruption, disrupting the individual poise and the unconscious tranquillity of the Infinite Soul with a recoil or tremendous shock which impregnated the unconsciousness of its apparent separateness from the indivisible state.

GOD SPEAKS–THE THEME OF CREATION AND ITS PURPOSE

Anne Bancroft (1931-2005)

Moments of true consciousness, unconditioned by the self, are usually fleeting but indelible. We always remember them. They remain to us as moments out of time.

It is a fallacy to believe that only the spiritually mature can experience such revelations. They do not come because one sits for many hours in meditation or prayer although, if that meditation softens and opens the hard core of self, they are there for the taking. But as gifts they are given to all—to young children as well as the very old, to the murderer as well as the monk, and for all we know to animals—to accept or to ignore.

WEAVERS OF WISDOM, WOMEN MYSTICS OF THE TWENTIETH CENTURY

Hubert Benoit (1904-1992)

He who would understand Zen should never lose sight of the fact that here it is essentially a question of the *sudden* doctrine. Zen, denying that man has any liberation to attain, or has to improve himself in any way, could not admit that his condition can improve little by little until it becomes normal at last. The satori-occurrence is only an instant between two periods of our temporal life; it may be likened to the line which separates a zone of shade from a zone of light, and it has no more real existence than this line. Either I do not see things as they are, or I see them; there is no period during which I should see little by little the Reality of the Universe.

THE SUPREME DOCTRINE

Richard Bucke (1337-1902)

All at once without any warning of any kind, I found myself wrapped in a flame-colored cloud. For an instant I thought of fire, an immense conflagration somewhere close by in the great city; the next, I knew that the fire was within myself. Directly afterward there came upon me a sense of exultation, of immense joyousness accompanied or immediately followed by an intellectual illumination impossible to describe. Among other things, I did not merely come to believe, but I saw that the universe is not composed of dead matter, but is, on the contrary, a living Presence; I became conscious in myself of eternal life. It was not a conviction that I would have eternal life, but a consciousness that I possessed eternal life then; I saw that all men are immortal; that the cosmic order is such that without any peradventure all things work together for the good of each and all; that the foundation principle of the world, of all worlds, is what we call love, and that happiness of each and all is in the long run absolutely certain. The vision lasted a few seconds and was gone; but the memory of it and the sense of reality of what it taught has remained during the quarter of a century which has since elapsed.

COSMIC CONSCIOUSNESS

Douglas Harding (1909-2007)

The best day of my life—my rebirthday, so to speak—was when I found I had no head. This is not a literary gambit, a witticism designed to arouse interest at any cost…. What actually happened was something absurdly simple and unspectacular: Just for the moment I stopped thinking. Reason and imagination and all mental chatter died down.

For once, words really failed me. I forgot my name, my humanness, my thingness, all that could be called me or mine. Past and future dropped away. It was as if I had been born that instant, brand-new, mindless, innocent of all memories. There existed only the Now, that present moment and what was clearly given in it. To look was enough. And what I found was khaki trouser legs terminating downward in a pair of brown shoes, khaki sleeves terminating sideways in a pair of pink hands, and a khaki shirtfront terminating upward in—absolutely nothing whatever! Certainly not in a head. It took me no time at all to notice that this nothing, this hole where a head should have been, was no ordinary vacancy, no mere nothing. On the contrary, it was very much occupied. It was a vast emptiness vastly filled, a nothing that found room for everything—room for grass, trees, shadowy distant hills, and far about them snowpeaks like a row of angular clouds riding the blue sky. I had lost a head and gained a world.... It felt like a sudden waking from the sleep of ordinary life, an end to dreaming.... *It was the revelation, at long last, of the perfectly obvious.*

ON HAVING NO HEAD

Kathleen Raine (1908-2003)

But here I had it, and sat like a bird on her nest, secure, unseen, part of the distance, with the world, day and night, wind and light, revolving round me in the sky. The distant and the near had no longer any difference between them, and I was in the whole, as far as my eyes could see, right to the sunset. The wind and the rain were like the boiling elements in a glass flask, that was the entire earth and sky held in my childish solipsist mind. The sun, the stratus clouds, the prevailing wind, the rustle of dry sedge, the western sky, were at one. Until the cold evening, or the rain, or the fear of the dark drove me to run home for safety to the less perfect, the human world, that I would enter, blinking as I came back into the light of the paraffin lamp in the kitchen.

FAREWELL HAPPY FIELDS

SCIENCE

Germaine de Staël (1766-1817)

Scientific progress makes moral progress a necessity; for if
man's power is increased, the checks that restrain him from
abusing it must be strengthened.

INFLUENCE OF LITERATURE UPON SOCIETY

Shivapuri Baba (1826-1963)

There should be no conflict between Science and Religion.
They are complementary. Science has taken Religion to be its
enemy which it should not. Practice of Right Life is a kind
of science. There is no harm if science is able to bring any
comfort to individuals and society. But science should not
attempt to override Divine laws, nor should it be used to gain
material wealth at the cost of social harmony.

Every religion is restricted by theories, arguments, blind faith, unnecessary and sometimes unwanted practices. Religion may at times create an atmosphere for good life, but it cannot fulfil the tasks ordained by God, nor can it by itself lead to God or Realization.

QUOTED IN *LONG PILGRIMAGE,* J. G. BENNETT

Carl Gustav Jung (1875-1961)

We must remember that the rationalistic attitude of the West is not the only possible one and is not all-embracing, but is in many ways a prejudice and a bias that ought perhaps to be corrected.... Causality...acquired its importance only in the course of the last two centuries, thanks to the leveling influence of the statistical method on the one hand and the unparalleled success of the natural sciences on the other, which brought the metaphysical view of the world into disrepute.

"SYNCHRONICITY: AN ACAUSAL CONNECTING PRINCIPLE," IN *THE INTERPRETATION OF NATURE AND THE PSYCHE*

Albert Einstein (1879-1955)

A conviction, akin to religious feeling, of the rationality or intelligibility of the world lies behind all scientific work of a higher order. This firm belief, a belief bound up with deep feeling, in a superior mind that reveals itself in the world of experience, represents my conception of God.

THE AMERICAN WEEKLY, 1948

Aldous Huxley (1894-1963)

Scientists simplify, they abstract, they eliminate all that, for their purposes, is irrelevant and ignore whatever they choose to regard as inessential; they impose a style, they compel the facts to verify a favorite hypothesis, they consign to the waste-paper basket all that, to their mind, falls short of perfection.

THE DOORS OF PERCEPTION

Martin Luther King, Jr. (1929-1968)

Our scientific power has outrun our spiritual power. We have guided missiles and misguided men.

STRENGTH TO LOVE

David Bohm (1917–1992)

The present state of theoretical physics implies that empty space has all this energy and that matter is a slight increase of that energy and therefore matter is like a small ripple on this tremendous ocean of energy, having some relative stability and being manifest.

Therefore my suggestion is that this implicate order implies a reality immensely beyond what we call matter. Matter itself is merely a ripple in this background.

DIALOGUES WITH SCIENTISTS AND SAGES: THE SEARCH FOR UNITY, RENÉE WEBER

Jacques Cousteau (1910–1997)

Scientists in their quest for certitude and proof tend to reject the marvelous.

QUOTED FROM *UNKNOWN MAN* BY YATRI

Arthur Eddington (1882-1944)

We see the atoms with their girdles of circulating electrons darting hither and thither, colliding and rebounding. Free electrons torn from the girdles hurry away a hundred times faster, curving sharply round the atoms with side-slips and hairbreadth escapes.... The spectacle is so fascinating that we have perhaps forgotten that there was a time when we wanted to be told what an electron is. The question was never answered.... *Something unknown is doing we don't know what*—that is what our theory amounts to. It does not sound a particularly illuminating theory. I have read something like it elsewhere...

There is the same suggestion of activity. There is the same indefiniteness as to the nature of the activity and of what it is that is acting.

THE NATURE OF THE PHYSICAL WORLD

Marilyn Ferguson (1938-2008)

From science and from the spiritual experience of millions, we are discovering our capacity for endless awakenings in a universe of endless surprises.

THE AQUARIAN CONSPIRACY

Lyall Watson (1939-2008)

As our knowledge grows there must be a million or more genes in our nuclei that we are just not using—we have enormous genetic deposit accounts on which we could presumably draw in times of need.

LIFE TIDE

SILENCE AND STILLNESS

Zen saying
Soundless and without scent, heaven and earth are
incessantly repeating unwritten sutras.

Lao Tzu (c. 6th Century BCE)
He who knows does not speak.
He who speaks does not know.
TAO TE CHING

The Way is unimpeded harmony; its potential may never
be fully exploited. It is as deep as the source of all things: It
blunts the edges, resolves the complications, harmonizes the

light, assimilates to the world. Profoundly still, it seems to be there: I don't know whose child it is, before the creation of images.

THE ESSENTIAL TAO, THOMAS CLEARY

The Bhagavad Gita (c. 500 CE)

The man who, casting off all desires, lives free from attachment; who is free from egoism and from the feeling that this or that is mine, obtains tranquillity.

The Dhammapada (3rd Century BCE)

All thy rafters are broken, thy ridge-pole is sundered; thy mind, approaching Nirvana, has attained to extinction all desires.

QUOTED FROM *THE SOUL: AN ARCHAEOLOGY*, CLAUDIA SETZER

Sosan (Seng-t'san)
The Third Zen Patriarch (c. 600)

Emptiness here, Emptiness there, but the infinite universe
stands always before your eyes.

DISCOURSES ON THE FAITH MIND; OR,
THE BOOK OF NOTHING (HSIN HSIN MING)

Old Testament

A man of understanding remains silent.

PROVERBS 11:12

Dyonysius (c. 6th Century)

The higher we soar in contemplation the more limited
become our expressions of that which is purely intelligible;
even as now, when plunging into the Darkness which is above
the intellect, we pass not merely into brevity of speech, but
even into absolute silence, of thoughts as well as of words…
and, according to the degree of transcendence, so our speech
is retrained until, the entire ascent being accomplished, we
become wholly voiceless, inasmuch as we are absorbed in
Him who is totally ineffable.

Otomo No Tabito (665-731)

To sit silent
And look wise
Is not to be compared with
Drinking saké
And making a riotous shouting.

SAYING

Wang Wei (699-761)

I have always been a lover of tranquillity
And when I see this clear stream so calm
I want to stay on some great rock
And fish for ever on and on.

"THE GREEN STREAM" IN *THE POEMS OF WANG WEI*

Shantideva (8th Century)

My mind will not experience peace
If it fosters painful thoughts of hatred.

A GUIDE TO THE BODHISATTVA'S WAY OF LIFE

Chia Tao (777-841)

I asked the boy beneath the pines.
He said, "The master's gone alone
Herb-picking somewhere on the mount,
Cloud-hidden, whereabouts unknown."

MY COUNTRY AND MY PEOPLE

Pao-tzu Wen-ch'I (c. 900)

Drinking tea, eating rice,
I pass my time as it comes;
Looking down at the stream,
Looking up at the mountain,
How serene and relaxed I feel indeed!

KOAN

Hakim Sanai (12th Century)

And if, my friend, you ask me the way [to God],
I'll tell you plainly, it is this:
to turn your face toward the world of life,
and turn your back on rank and reputation;
and, spurning outward prosperity, to bend
your back double in his service;
to part company with those who deal in words,
and take your place in the presence of the wordless.

THE WALLED GARDEN OF TRUTH

Marie de France (1160?–1215?)

Whoever has received knowledge and eloquence in speech
from God should not be silent or secretive but demonstrate
it willingly. When a great good is widely heard of, then, and
only then, does it bloom, and when that good is praised by
man, it has spread its blossoms.

LETTERS

Jalal al-Din Rumi (1207-1273)

But at the very least, by practising God's remembrance your inner being will be illuminated little by little and you will achieve some measure of detachment from the world.

TALES OF THE MATHNAWI

Meister Eckhart (1260-1327)

Only he to whom God is present in everything and who employs his reason in the highest degree and has enjoyment in it knows anything of true peace and has a real kingdom of heaven.

SERMONS

The Book of Common Prayer

The peace of God which passes all understanding.

HOLY COMMUNION: THE BLESSING

La Fontaine (1621-1695)

People who make no noise are dangerous.

FABLES

Thomas Carlyle (1795-1881)

Speech is of time, silence is of eternity

SARTOR RESARTUS

Alfred de Vigny (1797-1863)

Only silence is great; all else is weakness.

LA MORT DU LOUP

Ralph Waldo Emerson (1803-1882)

I like the silent church before the service begins, better than any preaching.

SELF-RELIANCE

A political victory, a rise in rents, the recovery of your sick, or the return of your absent friend, or some other quite external event, raises your spirits, and you think good days are preparing for you. Do not believe it. It can never be so. Nothing can bring you peace but yourself.

SELF-RELIANCE

Hazrat Inayat Khan (1882-1927)

The greatest fault of the day is the absence of stillness.
Stillness is nowadays often taken as leisureliness or as
slowness. Modern man lacks concentration and carries
with him an atmosphere of restlessness; with all his
knowledge and progress he feels uncomfortable himself,
and unintentionally brings discomfort to others. Stillness is
therefore the most important lesson that can be taught to
the youth of today.

THE SUFI MESSAGE OF HAZRAT INAYAT KHAN:
THE ART OF PERSONALITY

Kahlil Gibran (1883-1931)

Believe in the unsaid, for the silence of men is nearer the
truth than their words.

JESUS, THE SON OF MAN: HIS WORDS AND HIS DEEDS
AS TOLD AND RECORDED BY THOSE WHO KNEW HIM

Franz Kafka (1883-1924)

There is infinite hope, but not for us.

LETTERS

J. Krishnamurti (1895-1986)

The silence of the mind is the true religious mind, and the silence of the gods is the silence of the earth.

THE SECOND PENGUIN KRISHNAMURTI READER

John Cage (1912-1992)

We are involved in a life that passes understanding and our highest business is our daily life.

SILENCE

Try as we may to make a silence, we cannot.

SILENCE

Albert Camus (1913-1960)

In order to understand the world, one has to turn away from it on occasion; in order to serve men better, one has to hold them at a distance for a time. But where can one find the solitude necessary to vigor, the deep breath in which the mind collects itself and courage gauges its strength? There remain big cities.

THE MINOTAUR OR THE STOP IN ORAN

U. G. Krishnamurti (Contemporary)

Unless you are at peace with yourself, there cannot be peace around the world. When are you going to be at peace with yourself—next life? No chance. Wait, you will see. Even then there is no guarantee that your society will be peaceful. They will not be at peace. When you are at peace with yourself, that is the end of the story.

MIND IS A MYTH—DISQUIETING CONVERSATIONS WITH A MAN CALLED U. G.

Mother Teresa (1910-1997)

God is the friend of silence. Trees, flowers, grass grow in silence. See the stars, moon, and sun, how they move in silence.

FOR THE BROTHERHOOD OF MAN

Sogyal Rinpoche (1910-1997)

We believe in a personal, unique, and separate identity; but if we dare to examine it, we find that this identity depends entirely on an endless collection of things to prop it up: our name, our "biography," our partners, family, home, job, friends, credit . . .[sic] It is on their fragile and transient support that we rely for our security.... Without our familiar props, we are faced with just ourselves, a person we do not know, an unnerving stranger with whom we have been living all the time but we never really wanted to meet. Isn't that why we have tried to fill every moment of time with noise and activity, however boring or trivial, to ensure that we are never life in silence with this stranger on our own?

THE TIBETAN BOOK OF LIVING AND DYING

SIN

Old Testament

The soul that sinneth, it shall die.

EZEKIEL 18:4

There is not a just man upon earth, that doeth good, and sinneth not.

ECCLESIASTES 7:20

Be not ashamed to confess thy sins.

ECCLESIASTES 4:26

New Testament

If we say that we have no sin, we deceive ourselves.

I JOHN 1:8

Rejoice with me; for I have found my sheep which was lost.

I say unto you, that likewise joy shall be in heaven over one sinner that repenteth, more than over ninety and nine just persons, which need no repentance.

LUKE 15:6–7

Which man of you, having a hundred sheep, if he lose one of them, doth not leave the ninety and nine in the wilderness, and go after that which is lost, until he find it?

And when he hath found it, he layeth it on his shoulders, rejoicing.

LUKE 15:4–5

Saint Augustine (354-430)

A good conscience is the palace of Christ; the temple of the Holy Ghost; the paradise of delight, the standing Sabbath of the saints.

CONFESSIONS

Omar Khayyam (d. 1123)

Myself when young did eagerly frequent
Doctor and Saint, and heard great Argument
About it and about; but evermore
Came out by the same Door wherein I went.

RUBAIYAT

Jalal al-Din Rumi (1207–1273)

Whenever the self-opinionated man sees a sin committed by another, a fire blazes up in him straight out of Hell; he calls that pride the defense of the faith, not seeing in himself that spirit of arrogance. But defense of the faith has a different token, for out of that fire a whole world becomes green.

TALES OF THE MASNAVI

Saint Thomas Aquinas (1224/5–1274)

Three things are necessary for the salvation of man: to know what he ought to believe; to know what he ought to desire; and to know what he ought to do.

TWO PRECEPTS OF CHARITY

Christopher Marlowe (1564-1593)

I count religion but a childish toy,
And hold there is no sin but ignorance.

THE JEW OF MALTA

Judith Sargent Murray (1751-1820)

Religion is 'twixt God and my own soul,
Nor saint, nor sage, can boundless thought control.

*ESSAY—A SKETCH FOR THE GLEANER'S
RELIGIOUS SENTIMENT*

Oscar Wilde (1854-1900)

I couldn't help it. I can resist everything except temptation.

LADY WINDERMERE'S FAN

The only way to get rid of a temptation is to yield to it.

PICTURE OF DORIAN GRAY

Dorothy Parker (1893-1967)

Three highballs, and I think I'm St. Francis of Assisi.

JUST A LITTLE ONE

Phyllis McGinley (1905-1978)

Sin…has been made not only ugly but passé. People are no longer sinful, they are only immature or underprivileged or frightened or, more particularly, sick.

For the wonderful thing about saints is that they were *human*. They lost their tempers, got hungry, scolded God, were egotistical or testy or impatient in their turns, made mistakes and regretted them. Still they went on doggedly blundering toward Heaven. And they won sanctity partly by willing to be saints, not only because they encountered no temptation to be less.

THE WISDOM OF THE SAINTS

Osho (1931-1990)

One should never go against one's nature. That is the only sin.

DISCOURSES

Da Free John (1939–2008)

The New Testament declares that there is only one
unpardonable sin. Among all of the enumerated sins only one
is unpardonable: the denial of the Holy Spirit or the Spirit
of God. If that is the one unforgivable sin, then something
about that sin must epitomize sin itself. All the forgivable
sins must somehow be the lesser versions of this primary sin.
Therefore, sin itself has to do with our tendency to deny or
dissociate from the Spiritual Divine.

THE FIRE GOSPEL

SPIRIT

The Upanishads (c. 900-600 BCE)

Spirit is not born, nor deceases ever,
has not come from any, or from it any.
This Unborn, Eternal, and Everlasting
Ancient is not slain, be it slain the body.

KATHA UPANISHAD

The Bhagavad Gita (c. 500 BCE)

It is greedy desire and wrath, born of passion, the great evil,
the sum of destruction: This is the enemy of the soul.
These bodies are perishable; but the dwellers in these bodies
are eternal, indestructible, and impenetrable.
The soul which is not moved,

The soul that with a strong and constant calm,
Takes sorrow and takes joy indifferently,
Lives in the life undying.

QUOTED FROM *THE SOUL*: AN ARCHEOLOGY,
CLAUDIA SETZER

Socrates (469-399 BCE)

Are you not ashamed that you give your attention to
acquiring as much money as possible, and similarly with
reputation and honor, and give no attention or thought to
Truth and understanding, and the perfection of your soul?

Shall we believe that the soul, which is invisible, and
which goes hence to a place that is like herself, glorious, and
pure, and invisible, to Hades, which is rightly called the
unseen world to dwell with the good and wise God (whither,
if it be the will of God, my soul too must shortly go)—shall we
believe that the soul, whose nature is so glorious, and pure,
and invisible, is blown away by the winds and perishes as
soon as she leaves the body, as the world says?

PLATO'S PHAEDO

Hippocrates (c. 460-357 BCE)

The human soul develops up to the time of death.

APHORISMS

Heraclitus (c. 4th Century BCE)

You could not discover the frontiers of soul, even if you traveled every road to do so; such is the depth of its meaning.

CRATYLIS

Virgil (70-19 BCE)

The spirit within nourishes and the mind, diffused through all the members, sways the mass and mingles with the whole frame.

AENEID

Ovid (43 BCE-17 CE)

Those things that nature denied to human sight, she revealed to the eyes of the soul.

METAMORPHOSES

Seneca (c. 4 BCE–65 CE)

The soul alone raises us to nobility.

EPISTLES

Plotinus (204–270)

For the soul is the beginning of all things.
It is the soul that lends all things movement.

ENNEADS

Lucian (c. 240–312)

The wealth of the soul is the only true wealth.

DIALOGUES

Saint Ambrose (c. 340–397)

We know that it [the soul] survives the body and that being
set free from the bars of the body, it sees with clear gaze
those things which before, dwelling in the body, it could
not see.

HEXAMERON

Saint Augustine (354-430)

The life whereby we are joined into the body is called the soul.

QUOTED IN *THE SOUL: AN ARCHEOLOGY*, CLAUDIA SETZER

Solomon ben Judah ibn-Gabirol (c. 1021-1058)

The created soul is gifted with the knowledge which is proper to it; but after it is united to the body, it is withdrawn from receiving those impressions which are proper to it, by reason of the very darkness of the body.

FOUNTAIN OF LIFE

Jalal al-Din Rumi (1207-1273)

This body is a tent for the spirit, an ark for Noah.

UNTITLED

Juliana of Norwich (c. 1342-1417)

The soul,
that noble and joyful life
that is all peace and love,
draws the flesh to give its consent
by grace.
And both shall be one
in eternal happiness.
Our soul is one to God,
unchangeable goodness,
and therefore
between God and our soul
there is neither wrath nor forgiveness
because there is no between.
Because of the beautiful oneing
that was made by God
between the body and the soul
it must be
that we will be restored
from double death.

MEDITATIONS WITH JULIANA OF NORWICH

The soul has a ghostly spot in her where she has all things matter-free, just as the first cause harbors in itself all things with which it creates all things. The soul also has a light in her with which she creates all things. When this light and this spot coincide so that each is the seat of the other, then, only, one is in full possession of one's mind. What more is there to tell?

MEDITATIONS WITH JULIANA OF NORWICH

Marsilio Ficino (1433-1499)

The planets correspond, then, to deeply felt movements of the soul.

THEOLOGIA PLATONICA

Kabir (c. 1440-1518)

I laugh when I hear that the fish in the water is thirsty.
You don't grasp the fact that what is most alive of all is inside
  your own house;
and so you walk from one holy city to the next with a
  confused look!

Kabir will tell you the truth: go wherever you like, to
    Calcutta or Tibet,
if you can't find where your soul is hidden,
for you the world will never be real!
THE KABIR BOOK: FORTY-FOUR OF THE ECSTATIC
POEMS OF KABIR

Paracelsus (1493-1541)
Since nothing is so secret or hidden that it cannot be revealed,
everything depends on the discovery of those things that
manifest the hidden.
ESSENTIAL READINGS

Saint Teresa of Avila (1515-1582)
Accustom yourself continually to make many acts of love,
for they enkindle and melt the soul.
MAXIMS FOR HER NUNS

Remember that you have only one soul; that you have only one death to die; that you have only one life, which is short and has to be lived by you alone; and there is only one glory, which is eternal. If you do this, there will be many things about which you care nothing.

MAXIMS FOR HER NUNS

Michel de Montaigne (1533-1592)

Physicians might, I believe, make greater use of scents than they do, for I have often noticed that they cause changes in me, and act on my spirits according to their qualities; which make me agree with the theory that the introduction of incense and perfume into churches so ancient and widespread a practice among all nations and religions, was for the purpose of raising our spirits, and of exciting and purifying our senses, the better to fit us for contemplation.

ESSAYS

William Shakespeare (1564-1616)

O my prophetic soul!

HAMLET, I, 5, 40

I do not set my life at a pin's fee,
And for my soul, what can it do to that,
Being a thing immortal as itself?
HAMLET, I, 5, 65

Every subject's duty is the King's, but every subject's soul is
his own.
HENRY, V, IV, 1, 181

Be cheerful, Sir.
Our revels are now ended. These our actors,
As I foretold you, were all spirits, and
Are melted into air, into thin air:
And, like the baseless fabric of this vision,
The cloud-capp'd towers, the gorgeous palaces,
The solemn temples, the great globe itself,
Yea, all which it inherit, shall dissolve,
And, like this insubstantial pageant faded,
Leave not a rack behind. We are such stuff
As dreams are made on; and our little life
Is rounded with a sleep.
THE TEMPEST, IV i

Mr. Tut-Tut (c. 17th Century)

Who is narrow of vision cannot be bighearted; who is narrow of spirit cannot take long, easy strides.

ONE HUNDRED PROVERBS

Sarmad (17th Century)

Do not ask me questions on my way of life.
All writing is useless; useless is all interpretation;
All words and sentences are useless,
Unless the Spirit is ready to hear.

RUBAIYATS OF SARMAD 162

G. W. Leibniz (1646-1716)

The soul is the mirror of an indestructible universe.

THE MONADOLOGY

J. W. von Goethe (1749-1832)

Our spirit is a being of a nature quite indestructible and its activity continues from eternity to eternity. It is like the sun, which seems to set only to our earthly eyes, but which, in reality, never sets, but shines on unceasingly.

FAUST

William Blake (1757-1827)

Man has no body distinct from his soul; for that called body is a portion of the soul discern'd by the five senses, the chief inlets of soul in this age.

THE MARRIAGE OF HEAVEN AND HELL

J. C. Friedrich von Schiller (1759-1805)

A beautiful soul has no other merit than its own existence.

ÜBER ANMUT UND WÜRDE

Germaine de Staël (1766-1817)

The soul is the fire that darts its rays through all the senses; it is in this fire that existence consists; all the observations and all the efforts of the philosophers ought to turn toward this, the center and moving power of our sentiments and our ideas.

LETTERS

William Wordsworth (1770-1850)

Our birth is but a sleep and a forgetting;
The soul that rises with us, our life's star,
Hath had elsewhere its setting,
And cometh from afar.

QUOTED FROM *THE SOUL: AN ARCHEOLOGY*,
CLAUDIA SETZER

Percy Bysshe Shelley (1792-1822)

Throughout this varied and eternal world Soul is the only element.

QUEEN MAB

John Keats (1795–1821)
Call the world if you Please "The vale of Soul-making."
HYPERION

Ralph Waldo Emerson (1803–1882)
Before the revelations of the soul, Time and Space and
Nature shrink away.
NATURE

Elizabeth Blackwell (1821–1910)
As I draw near the borderland…the wonderful light of the
other life seems often to shine so joyfully into this one, that I
almost forget the past and present, in an eager anticipation of
the approaching awakening.
PIONEER WORK FOR WOMEN

Mary Baker Eddy (1821–1910)
Spirit is the real and eternal; matter is the unreal and temporal.
SCIENCE AND HEALTH WITH KEY TO THE SCRIPTURES

Sir Edward Burnett Tylor (1832–1917)

The act of breathing, so characteristic of the higher animals during life, and coinciding so closely with life in its departure, has been repeatedly and naturally identified with the life or soul itself….

ESSENTIAL SACRED WRITINGS FROM AROUND THE WORLD

Stéphane Mallarmé (1842–1898)

Every soul is a melody which needs renewing.

CRISE DE VERS

Sigmund Freud (1856–1939)

Man found that he was faced with the acceptance of "Spiritual" forces, that is to say such forces as cannot be apprehended by the senses, particularly not by sight, and yet having undoubted, even extremely strong effects…. The idea of the soul was thus born as the spiritual principle in the individual. Now the realm of spirits had opened for man, and he was ready to endow everything in nature with the soul he had discovered in himself.

"A PHILOSOPHY OF LIFE," IN NEW INTRODUCTORY LECTURES ON PSYCHOANALYSIS

Rabindranath Tagore (1861-1941)

That which oppresses me, is it my soul
trying to come out in the open,
or the soul of the world knocking
at my heart for its entrance?

SOUL CONSCIOUSNESS

Wassily Kandinsky (1866-1944)

There is nothing on earth so curious for beauty or so absorbent of it, as a soul.

RETROSPECT

Ramana Maharshi (1879-1950)

That inner Self, as the primeval Spirit, eternal, ever effulgent, full and infinite Bliss, single, indivisible, whole and living,

shines in everyone as the witnessing awareness. That Self
in its splendor, shining in the cavity of the heart…This Self is
neither born nor dies, it neither grows nor decays, nor does it
suffer any change. When a pot is broken, the space in it
is not, and similarly, when the body dies the Self in it
remains eternal.

COLLECTED WORKS, ARTHUR OSBORNE

Helen Keller (1880-1968)

It seems to me that there is in each of us a capacity to
comprehend the impressions and emotions which have been
experienced by mankind from the beginning. This inherited
capacity is a sort of sixth sense—a soul-sense which sees,
hears, feels, all in one.

THE STORY OF MY LIFE

Pierre Teilhard de Chardin (1881-1955)

Matter is the matrix of Spirit. Spirit is the higher state
of Matter.

THE HEART OF THE MATTER

Hazrat Inayat Khan (1882-1927)

Patience is never wasted; patience is a process through which a soul passes and becomes precious. Souls who have risen above the world's limitations and sorrows, the world's falseness and deception, they are the souls who have passed through patience.

THE SUFI MESSAGE OF HAZRAT INAYAT KHAN: THE ART OF PERSONALITY

Kahlil Gibran (1883-1931)

There is no depth beyond the soul of man, and the soul is the deep that calls unto itself; for there is no other voice to speak and there are no other ears to hear.

JESUS, THE SON OF MAN: HIS WORDS AND HIS DEEDS AS TOLD AND RECORDED BY THOSE WHO KNEW HIM

Franz Kafka (1883-1924)

It's eternity in a person that turns the crank handle.

LETTERS

Nikos Kazantzakis (1883-1957)

The soul of man is a flame, a bird of fire that leaps from bough to bough, from head to head, and that shouts: "I cannot stand still, I cannot be consumed, no one can quench me!"

THE SAVIOURS OF GOD

D. H. Lawrence (1885-1930)

Let us hesitate no longer to announce that the sensual passions and mysteries are equally sacred with the spiritual mysteries and passions. Who would deny it any more? The only thing unbearable is the degradation, the prostitution of the living mysteries in us. Let man only approach his own self with a deep respect, even reverence for all that the creative soul, the God-mystery within us, puts forth. Then we shall all be sound and free. Lewdness is hateful because it impairs our integrity and our proud being.

The creative spontaneous soul sends forth its promptings of desire and aspiration in us. These promptings are our true fate, which is our business to fulfil. A fate dictated from outside, from theory or from circumstance, is a false fate.

PHOENIX II

Paul Tillich (1886-1965)

The most intimate motions within the depths of our souls are
not completely our own. For they belong also to our friends,
to mankind, to the universe, and the Ground of all being, the
aim of our life.

THE SHAKING OF THE FOUNDATIONS

Edna St. Vincent Millay (1892-1950)

The world stands out on either side
No wider than the heart is wide;
Above the world is stretched the sky,
No higher than the soul is high.
The heart can push the sea and land
Farther away on either hand;
The soul can split the sky in two,
And let the face of God shine through.
But East and West will pinch the heart
That can not keep them pushed apart;
And he whose soul is flat—the sky
Will cave in on him by and by.

THE HEART OF SOUL

Simone Weil (1909-1943)

The danger is not lest the soul should doubt whether there is any bread, but lest, by a lie, it should persuade itself that it is not hungry.

QUOTED IN THE SOUL: AN ARCHEOLOGY,
CLAUDIA SETZER

Paul Zweig (1935-1984)

In short, the soul-journey resembles very much the sort of adventure one encounters in folklore and myth. According to archaic view, all men apparently had the chance to become a sort of Odysseus, whether they like it or not.

THE ADVENTURER

Raymond Carver (1939-1988)

Words lead to deeds…. They prepare the soul, make it ready, and move it to tenderness.

NO HEROICS, PLEASE

William Barratt (1913–1992)

Thus at the center of the self there is a hole and a mystery.
Our own soul is unknown to us.

DEATH OF THE SOUL: FROM DESCARTES
TO THE COMPUTER

Jean Shinoda Bolen (Contemporary)

While everyone has a different experience of what is soulful,
these experiences do share similar beginnings. We start by
giving ourselves permission to be soulful, to take seriously
this aspect of ourselves, our soul and our soul's needs.

WINDOWS OF THE SOUL, HANDBOOK FOR THE SOUL

Ray Charles (1930–2004)

Some people tell me I'd invented the sounds they called soul—
but I can't take any credit. Soul is just the way black folk sing
when they leave themselves alone.

TELEVISION INTERVIEW

Da Free John (1939-2008)

You are all spirits. It is not that you "have" a spirit. To have a spirit implies that you are spirit and that you are also something else. Human beings *are* spirits. Being a human being is one of the ways of being a spirit.

THE FIRE GOSPEL

Robert Fulghum (Contemporary)

For all my good intentions, there are days when things go wrong or I fall into old habits. When things are not going well, when I'm grumpy or mad, I'll realize that I've not been paying attention to my soul and I've not been following my best routine.

PAY ATTENTION, HANDBOOK FOR THE SOUL, EDS. RICHARD CARLSON AND BENJAMIN SHIELD

Thomas Moore (Contemporary)

Everyone should know that you can't live in any other way than by cultivating the soul.

CARE OF THE SOUL

Sogyal Rinpoche (Contemporary)

Recognizing who is and who is not a true master is a very subtle and demanding business; and in an age like ours, addicted to entertainment, easy answers, and quick fixes, the more sober and untheatrical attributes of spiritual mastery might very well go unnoticed. Our ideas about what holiness is, that it is pious, bland, and meek, may make us blind to the dynamic and sometimes exuberantly playful manifestation of the enlightened mind.

THE TIBETAN BOOK OF LIVING AND DYING

Sangharakshita (Contemporary)

It has been recognized even in the West (by Schopenhauer) that all great Art contains an element of self-transcendence akin to that which constitutes the quintessence of religion. When this element of self-transcendence is consciously cultivated in poetry, in music, or in painting and sculpture, instead of the element of mere sensuous appeal, Art ceases to be a form of sensuous indulgence and becomes a kind

of spiritual discipline, and the highest stages of aesthetic
contemplation become spiritual experiences.

THE PATH OF THE INNER LIFE

Alice Walker (Contemporary)

To such people, your color, your sex, your*self* make you an
object. But an object, strangely, perversely, with a soul. A soul.

"LIVING BY THE WORD," IN *SELECTED WRITINGS*

THE SPIRITUAL PATH

The Epic of Gilgamesh (3rd Millennium BCE)

May Shamash [the sun god] give you your heart's desire, may he let you see with your eyes the thing accomplished which your lips have spoken; may he open a path for you where it is blocked, and a road for your feet to tread. May he open the mountains for your crossing, and may the night time bring you the blessings of night, and Lugulbanada, your guardian god, stand beside you for victory. May you have victory in the battle as though you fought with a child.

Lao Tzu (c. 6th Century BCE)

Manifest plainness,

Embrace simplicity,

Reduce selfishness,

Have few desires.

TAO TE CHING

The Bhagavad Gita (c. 500 BCE)

For all those who come to me for shelter, however weak or
humble or sinful they may be—women or Vaisyas or Sudras—
they all reach the Path supreme.

In this world, aspirants may find enlightenment by
two different paths. For the contemplative is the path of
knowledge; for the active is the path of selfless action.

QUOTED IN *THE SOUL: AN ARCHEOLOGY,*
CLAUDIA SETZER

Socrates (469-399 BCE)

For I do nothing but go about persuading you all, old and young alike, not to take thought for your persons or your properties, but first and chiefly to care about the greatest improvements of the soul.

PLATO'S PHAEDO

Heraclitus (c. 4th Century BCE)

You can never step in the same river twice.

THE FRAGMENTS

Anonymous (8th Century)

Fate has swept our race away,
Taken warriors in their strength and led them
To the death that was waiting.

ANGLO SAXAN SONG

Hakim Sanai (12th Century)

Why, tell me, if what you seek
does not exist in any place,
do you propose to travel there on foot?
The road your self must journey on
lies in polishing the mirror of your heart.
It is not by rebellion and discord
that the heart's mirror is polished free
of the rust of hypocrisy and unbelief:
Your mirror is polished by your certitude,
—by the unalloyed purity of your faith.

THE WALLED GARDEN OF TRUTH

Jalal al-Din Rumi (1207-1273)

The spiritual path wrecks the body and afterward restores
it to health.
It destroys the house to unearth the treasure, and with that
treasure builds it better than before.

TALES OF THE MATHNAWI

If you are irritated by every rub,
how will your mirror be polished?

TALES OF THE MATHNAWI

Fakhruddin Iraqi (1213–1289)

Beloved, I sought You here and there,
Asked for news of You from all I met.
Then I saw You through myself,
And found we were identical.
Now I blush to think I ever searched
For signs of You.
By day I praised You, but never knew it;
By night I slept with You without realizing it,
Fancying myself to be myself;
But no, I was You and never knew it.

Kabir (c. 1440–1518)

Tell me, O Swan, your ancient tail.

From what land do you come, O Swan,

to what shore will you fly?

Where would you take your rest, O Swan,

and what do you seek?

Even this morning, O Swan,

Awake, arise, follow me!

There is a land where no doubt nor sorrow have rule:

Where the terror of Death is no more.

There the woods of spring are a-bloom,

And the fragrant scent "He is I" is borne on the wind:

There the Bee of the Heart

is deeply immersed, and desires no other joy.

THE ONE HUNDRED POEMS OF KABIR

Mira Bai (c. 1498–1546)

O my King,
I relish this loss of good name greatly.
Some will revile me, some will praise me,
But I shall follow my unfathomable path.
On this narrow path
I have met men of God.

PLAIN SPEAKING: DEVOTIONAL POEMS

Sarmad (17th Century)

The seeker of the Beloved finds Him
through quiet stillness, not in frantic activity.
That search is the purpose of life.

RUBAIYATS OF SARMAD 39

Mr. Tut-Tut (c. 17th Century)

Be firm in your acts, but easy in your heart; be strict with
yourself, but gentle with your fellow men.

ONE HUNDRED PROVERBS

God gives me bad luck, I meet it with a generous heart. God gives me labor and toil, I meet it with an easygoing mind. God gives me trials and adversities, I understand them by means of Tao.

ONE HUNDRED PROVERBS

John Henry Newman (1801-1890)

It is the saying of holy men that, if we wish to be perfect, we have nothing more to do than to perform the ordinary duties of the day well. A short road to perfection—short, not because easy, but because pertinent and intelligible. There are no short ways to perfection, but there are sure ones.

MEDITATIONS AND DEVOTIONS

George Moore (1852-1933)

A man travels the world over in search of what he needs and returns home to find it.

THE BROOK KERITH

Rabindranath Tagore (1861-1941)

Man's history is the history of his journey to the unknown in quest of the realization of his immortal self—his soul. Through the rise and fall of empires, through the building up of gigantic piles of wealth and the ruthless scattering of them upon the dust; through the creation of vast bodies of symbols that give shape to his dreams and aspirations, and the casting of them away like the playthings of an outworn infancy; through his forging of magic keys with which to unlock the mysteries of creation, and through his throwing away of this labor of ages to go back to his workshop and work up afresh some new form; yes, through it all man is marching from epoch to epoch toward the fullest realization of his soul,—the soul which is greater than the things man accumulates, the deeds he accomplishes, the theories he builds; the soul whose onward course is never checked by death or dissolution…. Yes, they are coming, the pilgrims, one and all—coming to their true inheritance of the world, they are ever broadening their consciousness, ever seeking a higher and higher unity, ever approaching nearer to the one central Truth which is all-comprehensive.

SOUL CONSCIOUSNESS

George Santayana (1863-1952)

Spirituality lies in regarding existence merely as a vehicle for contemplation, and contemplation merely as a vehicle for joy.

THREE PHILOSOPHICAL POETS

Sri Aurobindo (1872-1950)

The spiritual perfection which opens before man is the crown of long, patient, millennial outflowing of the Spirit in life and nature. This belief in a gradual spiritual progress and evolution is the secret of the almost universal Indian acceptance of the truth of reincarnation.

QUOTED FROM *THE SOUL: AN ARCHAEOLOGY*, CLAUDIA SETZER

Hermann Hesse (1877-1962)

When you throw a stone into the water, it finds the quickest way to the bottom of the water. It is the same when Siddhartha has an aim, a goal. Siddhartha does nothing; he waits, he thinks, he fasts, but he goes through the affairs of the world like a stone through water, without doing anything, without bestirring himself; he is drawn and lets himself fall. He is drawn by his goal, for he does not allow anything to enter his mind which opposes his goal…. It is what fools call magic and what they think is caused by demons. Nothing is caused by demons; there are no demons. Everyone can perform magic, everyone can reach his goal, if he can think, wait, and fast.

SIDDHARTHA

When someone is seeking…it happens quite easily that he only sees the thing that he is seeking; that he is unable to find anything, unable to absorb anything, because he is only thinking of the thing he is seeking, because he has a goal, because he is obsessed with his goal. Seeking means: to have a goal; but finding means: to be free, to be receptive, to have no goal.

SIDDHARTHA

Harry Emerson Fosdick (1878-1969)

If we hang beautiful pictures on the walls of our souls, mental images that establish us in the habitual companionship of the highest that we know, and live with them long enough, we cannot will evil.

THE HOPE OF THE WORLD

J. Krishnamurti (1895-1986)

So each of us must seek, so each one of us must dance through life, must have tremendous ecstasies, great sorrows and pains and great pleasures; and the greater and stronger they are, the more quickly shall we arrive at that stage of Nirvana, that absolute oneness with Life.

THE POOL OF WISDOM

Wilhelm Reich (1897-1957)

You think the goal justifies the means, even the vile means. You are wrong: *The goal is in the path on which you arrive at it. Every step of today is your life of tomorrow*. No great goal can be reached by vile means. That you have proven in every social revolution. The vileness or inhumanity of the path to the goal makes you vile or inhuman, and the goal unattainable.

LISTEN, LITTLE MAN!

Joseph Campbell (1904-1987)

Follow your bliss.

MOTTO

Alan Watts (1915-1973)

The central core of the [spiritual] experience seems to be the conviction, or insight, that the immediate *now*, whatever its nature, is the goal and fulfillment of all living. Surrounding and flowing from this insight is an emotional ecstasy, a sense of intense relief, freedom, and lightness, and often of almost unbearable love for the world, which is, however, secondary. Often, the pleasure of the experience is confused with the experience and the insight lost in the ecstasy, so that in trying to retain the secondary effects of the experience the individual misses its point—that the immediate *now* is complete even when it is not ecstatic. For ecstasy is a necessarily impermanent contrast in the constant fluctuation of our feelings. But insight, when clear enough, persists…. The terms in which a man interprets this experience are naturally drawn from the religious and philosophical ideas of his culture, and their differences often conceal its basic identity. As water seeks the course of least resistance, so the emotions clothe themselves in the symbols that lie most readily to hand, and the association is so swift and automatic that the symbol may appear to be the very heart of the experience.

THIS IS IT: AND OTHER ESSAYS ON ZEN AND SPIRITUAL EXPERIENCE

There was never a spiritual movement without its excesses and distortions.

THIS IS IT: AND OTHER ESSAYS ON ZEN AND SPIRITUAL EXPERIENCE

Osho (1931–1990)

Growth is a rare phenomenon. It is natural, yet rare. When the seed has found its right soil, it grows. It is very natural; growth is natural but to find the right soil—that is the very crux of the matter.

DISCOURSES

Hubert Benoit (1904–1992)

To the question "What must I do to free myself?" Zen replies: "There is nothing you need do since you have never been enslaved and since there is nothing in reality from which you can free yourself."

THE SUPREME DOCTRINE

Da Free John (1939-2008)

Turning in to a fully developed Master Field, where all of these evolutionary processes have already taken place, permits those changes to be magnified and quickened or, in effect, lived into that system without its having to pass through certain of the processes associated with the individual struggle to evolve.

Therefore, as I have indicated, the Spiritual Adept is a unique mechanism in Nature provided for the sake of the spiritual and altogether human evolution of human beings as well as the transformation and evolution of all beings and all processes that exist in the cosmos.

THE ENLIGHTENMENT OF THE WHOLE BODY

U. G. Krishnamurti (Contemporary)

There is no path of wisdom, there is no path at all. There is no journey.

THE MYSTIQUE OF ENLIGHTENMENT—THE UNRATIONAL IDEAS OF A MAN CALLED U .G.

Starhawk (Contemporary)

There is no dichotomy between spirit and flesh, no split between Godhead and the World.... Spiritual union is found in life within nature, passion, sensuality—through being fully human, fully one's self.

QUOTED FROM *THE SOUL: AN ARCHAEOLOGY,* CLAUDIA SETZER

TIME

Virgil (70-19 BCE)

Time bears away all things—even our minds.

ECLOGUES

Plotinus (203-262)

Time was not yet;…it lay…merged in the eternally Existent and motionless with It. But an active principle there…stirred from the rest;…for the One contained an unquiet faculty,… and it could not bear to retain within itself all the dense fullness of its possession.

Like a seed at rest, the nature-principle within, unfolding outward, makes its way toward what appears a multiple life. It was Unity self-contained, but now, in going forth from Itself, It fritters Its unity away; It advances to a lesser greatness.

Sosan (Seng-s'tan)
The Third Zen Patriarch (c. 600)

Words!

The way is beyond language,

for in it there is

no yesterday

no tomorrow

no today.

HSIN HSIN MING—DISCOURSES ON THE FAITH MIND OR
THE BOOK OF NOTHING

Huang Po (800–850)

Beginningless time and the present moment are the same....
You have only to understand that time has no real existence.

THE ZEN TEACHINGS OF HUANG-PO

Omar Khayyam (d. 1123)

Ah, fill the cup: What boots it to repeat
how time is slipping underneath our feet:
Unborn tomorrow and dead yesterday,
Why fret about them if today be sweet!
One moment in annihilation's waste,
One moment, of the well of life to taste—
The stars are setting and the caravan
Starts for the Dawn of Nothing—Oh, make haste!

RUBAIYAT

Meister Eckhart (1260-c. 1329)

It is an obvious fact that time affects neither God nor the soul.
Did time touch the soul she would not be the soul. If God
were affected by time he would not be God. Further, if time
could touch the soul, then God could not be born in her. The
soul wherein God is born must have escaped from time, and
time must have dropped away from her.

MEDITATIONS

William Shakespeare (1564-1616)

To-morrow, and to-morrow, and to-morrow,
Creeps in this petty pace from day to day
To the last syllable of recorded time,
And all our yesterdays have lighted fools
The way to dusty death. Out, out, brief candle!
Life's but a walking shadow, a poor player,
That struts and frets his hour upon the stage,
And then is heard no more; it is a tale
Told by an idiot, full of sound and fury,
Signifying nothing.

MACBETH

Matsuo Basho (1644-1694)

The months and days are the travelers of eternity. The years
that come and go are also voyagers.... I, too, for years past
have been stirred by the sight of a solitary cloud drifting with
the wind to ceaseless thoughts of roaming.

THE NARROW ROAD TO THE DEEP NORTH

Thomas Carlyle (1795-1881)

In the midst of winter, I finally learned that there was in me an invincible summer.

ON THE CHOICE OF BOOKS

Rudolf Steiner (1861-1925)

Thus there are these two streams, one from the past and one from the future, which come together in the soul—will anyone who observes himself deny that?

METAMORPHOSES OF THE SOUL

J. Krishnamurti (1895-1986)

In the now is all time, and to understand the now is to be free of time. Becoming is the continuation of time, of sorrow. Becoming does not contain being. Being is always in the present, and being is the highest form of transformation.

COMMENTARIES ON LIVING—FROM THE NOTEBOOKS OF J.KRISHNAMURTI

Arthur Bryant (1899-1985)

Rightly conceived, time is the friend of all who are in any way in adversity, for its mazy road winds in and out of the shadows sooner or later into sunshine, and when one is at its darkest point one can be certain that presently it will grow brighter.

Wei Wu Wei (1895-1986)

It was true before he said it, it is true at this moment, and it will be true forever, for there is no time.

OPEN SECRET

Marie-Louise von Franz (1915-1998)

In man's original point of view time was life itself and its divine mystery.

TIME: RHYTHM AND REPOSE

TRUTH

The Upanishads (c. 900-600 BCE)

The Person of a thumb in size
within one's very self abides;
The Lord of past and of future,
from Him, when once he's know, none hides
This verily is That.

KATHA UPANISHAD

Confucius (551-479 BCE)

Truth may not depart form human nature.
If what is regarded as truth departs from human nature,
it may not be regarded as truth.

THE APHORISMS OF CONFUCIUS, VI,
"HUMANISM AND TRUE MANHOOD"

Menander (c. 342–292 BCE)

The truth sometimes not sought for comes forth to the light.

THE QUESTIONS OF MILINDA

Saraha (1st or 2nd Century)

When the deluded in a mirror look
They see a face, not a reflection.
So the mind that has truth denied
Relies on that which is not true.

THE ROYAL SONG OF SARAHA

Martin Luther (1483–1546)

Here I stand, I cannot do otherwise.

SPEECH, DIET OF WORMS, 1521

Michel de Montaigne (1533–1592)

But truth is so great a thing that we ought not to despise
any medium that will conduct us to it.

ESSAYS

[Truth] must be loved for its own sake. A man who speaks the truth because he is in some way compelled or for his own advantage, and who is not afraid to tell a lie when it is of no importance to anyone, is not truthful enough. My soul naturally shuns a lie, and hates even the thought of one. I feel an inward shame and a sharp remorse if an untruth happens to escape me—as sometimes it does if the occasion is unexpected, and I am taken unawares.

ESSAYS

Sir Francis Bacon (1561-1626)

There are and can be only two ways of searching into and discovering truth. The one flies from the senses and particulars to the most general axioms…this way is now in fashion. The other derives axioms from the senses and particulars, rising by a gradual and unbroken ascent, so that it arrives at the most general axioms last of all. This is the true way but as yet untried.

NOVUM ORGANUM

Be so true to thyself, as thou be not false to others.

"OF WISDOM FOR A MAN'S SELF," IN *ESSAYS*

Sir Isaac Newton (1642-1727)

I do not know what I may appear to the world, but to myself
I seem to have been a boy playing on the seashore, and
diverting myself in now and then finding a smoother pebble,
or a prettier shell than ordinary, whilst the great ocean of
truth lay all undiscovered before me.

LETTERS

Charlotte Lennox (1720-1804)

The only Excellence of Falsehood…is its Resemblance
to Truth….

ARABELLA; OR, THE FEMALE QUIXOTE

Henry David Thoreau (1817-1862)

It takes two to speak the truth,—one to speak, and another
to hear.

SPOKEN

Oscar Wilde (1854-1900)

The truth is rarely pure, and never simple.

LETTERS

J. Krishnamurti (1895-1986)

There is no path to truth. Truth must be discovered, but there is no formula for its discovery. What is formulated is not true. You must set out on the uncharted sea, and the uncharted sea is yourself.

COMMENTARIES ON LIVING—FROM THE NOTEBOOKS OF J. KRISHNAMURTI

Albert Camus (1913-1960)

I have never seen anyone die for the ontological argument. Galileo who held a scientific truth of great importance abjured it with the greatest ease as soon as it endangered his life. In a certain sense, he did right.

THE MYTH OF SISYPHUS

Osho (1931-1990)

When you argue, you assert. Assertion is violence, aggression, and the truth cannot be known by an aggressive mind, the truth cannot be discovered by violence.

DISCOURSES

Hubert Benoit (1904-1992)

Do not try to find the truth,
Merely cease to cherish opinions,
Tarry not in dualism.

INSCRIBED ON THE BELIEVING MIND AS QUOTED IN
HUBERT BENOIT *THE SUPREME DOCTRINE*

UNDERSTANDING

The Upanishads (c. 900-600 BCE)

But he who has no understanding,
aye mindful, full of stains,
Never reaches that abode,
only repeated birth obtains.
But he who is with understanding,
ever mindful, free from stain,
Verily reaches that abode
From which he is not born again.

KATHA UPANISHAD

Confucius (551-479 BCE)

The superior man understands what is right; the inferior man understands what will sell.

THE APHORISMS OF CONFUCIUS, VII, "THE SUPERIOR MAN AND THE INFERIOR MAN"

Demosthenes (c. 384-322 BCE)

You cannot have a proud and chivalrous spirit if your conduct is mean and paltry; for whatever a man's actions are, such must be his spirit.

THIRD OLYNTHIAC

Mencius (372-289 BCE)

Never has a man who has bent himself been able to make others straight.

BOOK III

The path of duty lies in what is near, and man seeks for it in what is remote.

BOOK IV

Søren Kierkegaard (1813-1855)

Life can only be understood backward, but it must be lived forward.

LIFE

D. H. Lawrence (1885-1930)

I know I am compound of two waves, I, who am temporal and mortal. When I am timeless and absolute, all duality has vanished. But whilst I am temporal and mortal, I am framed in the struggle and embrace of the two opposite waves of darkness and of light.

PHOENIX II

Lusin (d. 1936)

When you talk with famous scholars, the best thing is to pretend that occasionally you do not quite understand them. If you understand too little, you will be despised; if you understand too much, you will be disliked; if you just fail occasionally to understand them, you will suit each other very well.

THE EPIGRAMS OF LUSIN

J. Krishnamurti (1895-1986)

If we can really understand the problem, the answer will come out of it, because the answer is not separate from the problem.

THE PENGUIN KRISHNAMURTI READER

Ignorance is the lack of self-awareness; and knowledge is ignorance when there is no understanding of the ways of the self. Understanding of the self is freedom from knowledge.

COMMENTARIES ON LIVING—FROM THE NOTEBOOKS OF J. KRISHNAMURTI

To understand intellectually is not to understand at all.

COMMENTARIES ON LIVING—FROM THE NOTEBOOKS OF J. KRISHNAMURTI

Wei Wu Wei (1895-1986)

There is no need to read books, chant Sutras, recite Scriptures, perform any antics; there is nothing whatever to discuss, argue about, or explain.

There is nothing whatever to teach or to be learned. Every living (sentient) being knows this and is free to become aware of it and to "live" it.

OPEN SECRET

Osho (1931-1990)

Life is always moving into the unknown, and you are afraid. You want life to go according to your mind, according to the known, but life cannot follow you. It always moves into the unknown. That is why we are afraid of life, and whenever we get any chance we try to fix it because with the fixed, prediction is possible.

DISCOURSES

Da Free John (1939-2008)

The man of understanding is not entranced. He is not elsewhere. He is not having an experience. He is not passionless and inoffensive. He is awake. He is present. He knows no obstruction in the form of mind, identity, differentiation, and desire. He uses mind, identity, differentiation, and desire. He is passionate. His quality is an offence to those who are entranced, elsewhere, contained in the mechanics of experience, asleep, living as various forms of identity.

ENLIGHTENMENT OF THE WHOLE BODY

U. G. Krishnamurti (Contemporary)

When once you have understood that there is nothing to understand, what is there to communicate? Communication is just not necessary, so there is no point in discussing the possibility of communication. Your desire to communicate is part of your general strategy of achievement. Veiled behind that desire for communication is the dependency upon some outside power to solve your problems for you.

MIND IS A MYTH—DISQUIETING CONVERSATIONS WITH A MAN CALLED U .G.

Russell Schweichart (Contemporary)

You become startlingly aware how artificial are the thousands of boundaries we've created to separate and define. And for the first time in your life you feel in your gut the precious unity of the earth and of all living things it supports. The dissonance between this unity you see and the separateness of human groupings that you know exist is starkly apparent.

ON RETURN FROM AN APOLLO MISSION

VIRTUE

Anonymous

Go placidly amid the noise and haste and remember what
peace there may be in silence.

As far as possible without surrender be on good terms
with all persons.

Speak your truth quietly and clearly and listen to others,
even the dull and ignorant; they, too, have their story.

Avoid loud and aggressive persons, they are vexations to
the spirit.

If you compare yourself with others, you may become
vain and bitter for always there will be greater and lesser
persons than yourself. Enjoy your achievements as well as
your plans.

Keep interested in your own career, however humble; it is a real possession in the changing fortunes of time.

Exercise caution in your business affairs; for the world is full of trickery.

But let this not blind you to what virtue there is; many persons strive for high ideals; and everywhere life if full of heroism.

Be careful.

Strive to be happy.

DESIDERATA

Ancient Babylonia (Inscribed c. 650 bce)

Slander not, but speak kindness;

Speak not evil, but show goodwill;

Who slanders and speaks evil—

Unto him will Shamash requite it by…his head.

Open not wide thy mouth, guard thy lips;

If thou art provoked, speak not at once;

If thou speakest hastily, thou shalt afterward have to
    atone therefor;
Soothe (rather) thy spirit with silence.
Offer daily unto thy god
Sacrifice, prayer, the incense most meet (for the Deity):
Before thy god shalt thou have a heart of purity.
SUMERIAN ETHICAL FRAGMENT

Lao Tzu (c. 6th Century BCE)

Do nondoing, strive for nonstriving, savor the flavorless,
regard the small as important, make much of little, repay
enmity with virtue; plan for difficulty when it is still easy, do
the great while it is still small.

    The most difficult things in the world must be done while
they are easy; the greatest things in the world must be done
while they are small.

TAO TE CHING

Superior virtue is not conscious of itself as virtue, and so really is virtue. Inferior virtue cannot let go of being virtuous, and so is not virtue. Superior virtue does not seem to be busy, and yet there is nothing which it does not accomplish. Inferior virtue is always busy, and yet in the end leaves things undone.

TAO TE CHING

Be humble and you will remain entire. The sage does not display himself, therefore he shines. He does not approve himself therefore he is noted. He does not praise himself, therefore he has merit. He does not glory in himself, therefore he excels.

TAO TE CHING

Confucius (551-479 BCE)

The firm, the enduring, the simple, and the modest are near to virtue.

ANALECTS

Aesop (c. 550 BCE)

No act of kindness, no matter how small, is ever wasted.

THE LION AND THE MOUSE

Mencius (372-289 BCE)

Benevolence is the tranquil habitation of man, and righteousness is his straight path.

BOOK IV

Sincerity is the way of heaven.

BOOK IV

Water indeed will flow indifferently to the east or west, but will it flow indifferently up or down? The tendency of man's nature to good is like the tendency of water to flow downward. There are none but have this tendency to good, just as all water flows downward.

BOOK VI

Hroswitha of Gandersheim (c. 935-1000)

I know that it is as wrong to deny a divine gift as to pretend
falsely that we have received it.

UNTITLED

Jami (1414-1492)

Never preen yourself
that you are prideless:
for pride is more invisible
than an ant's footprint
on a black stone
in the dark of night.

THE ABODE OF SPRING

John Milton (1608-1674)

I cannot praise a fugitive and cloistered virtue, unexercised
and unbreathed, that never sallies out and sees her adversary,
but slinks out of the race, where that immortal garland is to
be run for, not without dust and heat.

AREOPAGITICA

Samuel Butler (1612-1680)

Absolute virtue is as sure to kill a man as absolute vice is, let alone the dullness of it and the pomposities of it.

NOTEBOOKS

Molière (1622-1673)

I prefer an accommodating vice to an obstinate virtue.

AMPHITRYON

Adam Lindsay Gordon (1833-1870)

Life is mostly froth and bubble,
Two things stand like stone,
Kindness in another's trouble,
Courage in your own.

YE WEARIE WAYFARER

Rudyard Kipling (1865-1936)

If you can keep your head when all about you
Are losing theirs and blaming it on you.

If you can trust yourself when all men doubt you
And make allowance for their doubting, too.

IF

Mohandas K. Gandhi (1869-1948)

I am not a visionary. I claim to be a practical idealist. The religion of nonviolence is not meant merely for the rishis [holy men] and saints. It is meant for the common people as well. Nonviolence is the law of our species as violence is the law of the brute. The spirit lies dormant in the brute and he knows no law but that of physical might. The dignity of man requires obedience to a higher law—the strength of the spirit.... Nonviolence in its dynamic condition means conscious suffering. It does not mean meek submission to the will of the evildoer, but it means the pitting of one's whole soul against the will of the tyrant. Working under this law of our being, it is possible for a single individual to defy the whole might of an unjust empire to save his honor, his religion, his soul and lay the foundation for that empire's fall or its regeneration.

"STATEMENTS ON NON-VIOLENCE,"
PUBLISHED IN *YOUNG INDIA*

Hazrat Inayat Khan (1882-1927)

Virtues are virtues because they give joy once they are practiced. If a virtue does not give joy, it is not a virtue.

THE SUFI MESSAGE OF HAZRAT INAYAT KHAN: THE ART OF PERSONALITY

Consideration is the greatest of all virtues, for in consideration all virtues are born. Veneration for God, courtesy toward others, respect of those who deserve it, kindness to those who are weak and feeble, sympathy with those who need it, all these come from consideration.

THE SUFI MESSAGE OF HAZRAT INAYAT KHAN: THE ART OF PERSONALITY

Osho (1931-1990)

The question is not of finding in your thoughts what is right and what is wrong, in your actions what is right and what is wrong. The question is of finding a consciousness so total and so intense that only whatever is right remains, and whatever is false burns out. You don't have to decide.

DISCOURSES

VISION

Quintus Ennis (239-169 BCE)

No one regards what is before his feet; we all gaze at the stars.

DE DIVINATIONE

Shankara (788-820)

When the vision of Reality comes, the veil of ignorance is
completely removed. As long as we perceive things falsely,
our false perception distracts us and makes us miserable.
When our false perception is corrected, misery ends also.

CREST-JEWEL OF DISCRIMINATION

Kabir (c. 1440-1518)

I sell mirrors in the city of the blind.

THE ONE HUNDRED POEMS OF KABIR

Machiavelli (1469-1527)

All armed prophets have been victorious, and all unarmed prophets have been destroyed.

THE PRINCE

Mira Bai (1498-1546)

She drinks the honey of her vision.

DEVOTIONAL POEMS

William Shakespeare (1564-1616)

It adds a precious seeing to the eye.

LOVE'S LABOR'S LOST, IV, 3, 332

Argus, all eyes and no sight.

TROILUS AND CRESSIDA, I, 2, 20

William Blake (1757-1827)

A fool sees not the same tree that a wise man sees.

THE MARRIAGE OF HEAVEN AND HELL

Frederick Langbridge (1849-1923)

Two men look out through the same bars: One sees the mud, and one the stars.

CLUSTER OF QUIET THOUGHTS

Oscar Wilde (1854-1900)

We are all in the gutter, but some of us are looking at the stars.

LADY WINDERMERE'S FAN

Sigmund Freud (1856-1939)

When the wayfarer whistles in the dark, he may be disavowing his timidity, but he does not see any the more clearly for doing so.

THE PROBLEM OF ANXIETY

Yogaswami (1872-1964)

It is not a question of analyzing yourself. It is a question of seeing yourself.

POSITIVE THOUGHTS FOR DAILY MEDITATION

Will Rogers (1879-1935)

The fellow that can only see a week ahead is always the popular fellow, for he is looking with the crowd. But the one that can see years ahead, he has a telescope but he can't make anybody believe that he has it.

THE AUTOBIOGRAPHY OF WILL ROGERS

Edward de Bono (Contemporary)

A vision sets direction for thinking and action.

LATERAL THINKING

WISDOM

Lao Tzu (c. 6th Century BCE)

A wise man has no extensive knowledge.

He who has extensive knowledge is not a wise man.

The sage does not accumulate for himself.

The more he uses for others, the more he has himself.

The more he gives to others, the more he possesses of
    his own.

The Way of Heaven is to benefit others and not to injury.

The Way of the sage is to act but not to compete.

TAO TE CHING

Knowledge studies others,

Wisdom is self-known.

TAO TE CHING

Confucius (551–479 BCE)

"How dare I allow myself to be taken as sage and humane!" he said. "It may rather be said of me that I strive to become such without ceasing."

ANALECTS

The Bhagavad Gita (c. 500 BCE)

Even as all waters flow into the ocean, but the ocean never
overflows, even so the sage feels desires, but he is ever
one in his infinite peace.

Humility, unostentatiousness, non-injuring,

Forgiveness, simplicity, purity, steadfastness,

Self-control; this is declared to be wisdom;

What is opposed to this is ignorance.

Chuang Tzu (369-286 BCE)

For sacrifices to the River God, neither bulls with white foreheads, nor pigs with high snouts, nor men suffering from piles, can be used. This is known to all the soothsayers, for these are regarded as inauspicious. The wise, however, would regard them as extremely auspicious.

THIS HUMAN WORLD

The Gemara (c. 500)

The highest wisdom is kindness.

THE TALMUD

Sutra Kritanga (c. 500)

This is the quintessence of wisdom: not to kill anything.

Huang Po (800-850)

The foolish reject what they see, not what they think; the wise reject what they think, not what they see…. Observe things as they are and don't pay attention to other people.

THE ZEN TEACHINGS OF HUANG PO

Nicholas of Cusa (1401-1464)

Wisdom shining in all things invites us, with a certain foretaste of its effects, to be borne to its effects, to be borne to it with a wonderful desire. For life itself is an intellectual Spirit, having in itself a certain innate foretaste through which it searches with great desire for the very Font of its own life.

ON LEARNED IGNORANCE

Marguerite of Navarre (1492-1549)

Man is wise…when he recognizes no greater enemy than himself….

THE HEPTAMERON, OR NOVELS OF
THE QUEEN OF NAVARRE

Fools live longer than the wise, unless someone kills them… for…fools do not dissemble their passions. If they are angry they strike; if they are merry they laugh; but those who deem themselves wise hide their defects with so much care that their hearts are all poisoned with them.

THE HEPTAMERON, OR NOVELS OF
THE QUEEN OF NAVARRE

Catherine Willoughby (1519-1580)

Undoubtedly the greatest wisdom is not to be too wise.

LETTER TO WILLIAM CECIL

The Book of Common Prayer

The fear of the Lord is the beginning of wisdom.

Mr. Tut-Tut (c. 17th Century)

Personal talent coupled with a slow temper becomes great talent; wisdom coupled with a pacifist mind becomes true wisdom.

ONE HUNDRED PROVERBS

Edward Young (1683-1765)

Be wise with speed;
A fool at forty is a fool indeed.

NIGHT THOUGHTS

Mary Wortley Montagu (1689-1762)

People are never so near playing the fool as when they think themselves wise.

LETTER TO COUNTESS OF BUTE

Shneur Zalman of Liady (1747-1813)

The middle course [to reach perfection] is attainable by every individual; each person should try to reach it. A person who pursues the middle course does not despise the evil, which depends on the heart, and the times are not always conducive to such sentiments. But such a person is called on to depart from evil and do good through his behavior, in deed, word, and thought.... Therefore, let him delight in God, praised be he, by contemplating the greatness of the Eternal to the full extent of his capacities. Even though he recognizes that he will not reach this to its ultimate depth, but only by approximation, it is incumbent upon him to do what he can.

TANYA

John Ruskin (1819-1900)

And be sure also, if the author is worth anything, that you will not get at his meaning all at once—nay, that at his whole meaning you will not for a long time arrive in any wise. Not that he does not say what he means, and in strong words, too; but he cannot say it all and what is more strange, will not, but in a hidden way and in parable, in order that he may be sure you want it. I cannot see quite the reason of this, nor analyze that cruel reticence in the breasts of wise men which makes them always hide their deeper thought. They do not give it by way of help, but of reward, and will make themselves sure that you deserve it before they allow you to reach it.

HANDWRITTEN ON FRONT PAGE OF *ALL AND EVERYTHING*, G. I. GURDJIEFF

Laurence Hope (1865-1904)

For this is wisdom: to love, to live,
To take what Fate, or the Gods, may give.

"THE TEAK FOREST" IN *INDIA'S LOVE LYRICS*

Z'ev ben Shimon Halevi (Contemporary)

All complete religions have two faces. The outer facet takes
the form of words and public ritual, while the inner aspect
is the internal, often an oral instruction which is passed
on from teacher to pupil, who face-to-face have a personal
rapport in which the Master knows what and when it can be
taught to further the disciple's development. When the pupil
becomes a master in his own right he in turn imparts his own
wisdom and understanding to the next generation; so that
without a break a Tradition may be carried on over several
thousand years, without a trace of its outward appearance.

THE TREE OF LIFE

WORLD

Ptah-Hotep (c. 2600 BCE)

If thou art powerful, respect knowledge and calmness of
language. Command only to direct; to be absolute is to run
into evil. Let not thy heart be haughty, neither let it be mean.
Do not let thy orders remain unsaid and cause thy answers
to penetrate; but speak without heat, assume a serious
countenance. As for the vivacity of an ardent heart, temper
it; the gentle man penetrates all obstacles. He who agitates
himself all the day long has not a good moment; and he who
amuses himself all the day long keeps not his fortune.

THE BOOK OF PTAH-HOTEP, TRANSLATED IN THE
SACRED BOOKS AND EARLY LITERATURE OF THE EAST

The Upanishads (c. 900-600 BCE)

Now indeed there are three worlds—the world of men, the world of the ancestors, the world of the gods. This world of men here is to be gained only by a son and by no other means, the world of the ancestors by rites, the world of the gods by meditation. The world of the gods verily is the best of the worlds, therefore they praise meditation.

BRHAD UPANISHAD

Homeric Hymn (7th Century BCE)

I will sing of well-founded Gaia, Mother of All, eldest of all beings, she feeds all creatures that are in the world, all that go upon the goodly land and all that are in the paths of the sea, and all that fly: These are fed of her store.

Lao Tzu (c. 6th Century BCE)

The utility of a house depends on the empty spaces.
Thus, while the existence of things may be good, it is the nonexistent in them which makes them serviceable.

TAO TE CHING

Those who would take over the earth
And shape it to their will
Never, I notice, succeed.
The earth is like a vessel so sacred
That at the mere approach of the profane it is marred.
They reach out their fingers and it is gone.

TAO TE CHING

Put away holiness, throw away knowledge: thus the people
will profit a hundredfold. Put away morality, throw away
duty: thus the people will return to filial duty and love. Put
away skillfulness, throw away gain, and there will no longer
be thieves and robbers. In these three things beautiful
appearance is not enough. Therefore take care that men
have something to hold on to. Show simplicity, hold fast to
honesty! Give up learnedness! Thus you shall become free
of sorrows.

TAO TE CHING

The Bhagavad Gita (c. 500 BCE)

Whenever there is a withering of the Law and an uprising
of lawlessness on all sides, then I manifest Myself. For the
salvation of the righteous and the destruction of such as do
evil, I come to birth age after age.

KRISHNA TO ARJUNA AS QUOTED IN *THE SOUL:
AN ARCHEOLOGY*, CLAUDIA SETZER

Motse (c. 468–401 BCE)

Wu Matse said to Motse: "For all the righteousness that you
do, men do not help you and ghosts [spirits] do not bless you.
Yet you keep on doing it. You must be demented." Motse said:
"Suppose you have here two employees. One of them works
when he sees you but will not work when he does not see
you. The other one works whether he sees you or not. Which
of the two would you value?" Wu Matse said that he would
value him that worked whether he saw him or not. Motse
then said: "Then you are valuing him who is demented."

KENG CHU

Rabi'a al-Adawiyya (717-809)

I spun some yarn to sell for food
And sold it for two silver coins.
I put a coin in each hand
Because I was afraid
That if I put both together in one hand
This great pile of wealth might hold me back.

DOORKEEPER OF THE HEART

One day Rabi'a was sick,
And so her holy friends came to visit her, sat by her bedside,
And began putting down the world.
"You must be pretty interested in this 'world,'" said Rabi'a,
"otherwise—you wouldn't talk about it so much:
Whoever breaks the merchandise
Has to have bought it first."

DOORKEEPER OF THE HEART

Héloïse (c. 1098-1164)

Riches and power are but gifts of blind fate, whereas
goodness is the result of one's own merits.

LETTERS

Farid ud-Din Attar (1120?-1193?)

This love is not divine; it is mere greed
For flesh—an animal, instinctive need.

How long then will you seek for beauty here?
Seek the unseen, and beauty will appear

THE CONFERENCE OF THE BIRDS

Jalal al-Din Rumi (1207-1273)

Know, my son, that this whole world is a pitcher filled to the
brim with wisdom and beauty. The world is a single drop of
the Tigris [a river of present-day Iraq] of God's beauty which
on account of its fullness cannot be contained within
any vessel.

TALES OF THE MASNAVI

Jami (1414-1492)

Justice without religion is better for the order of the universe than the tyranny of a pious prince.

THE ABODE OF SPRING

Martin Luther (1483-1546)

War is the greatest plague that can afflict humanity; it destroys religion, it destroys states, it destroys families. Any scourge is preferable to it.

TABLE TALK

Mr. Tut-Tut (c. 17th Century)

All the universe is an inn; search not specially for a retreat of peace: all the people are your relatives; expect therefore troubles from them.

ONE HUNDRED PROVERBS

Sir William Jones (1746-1794)

My opinion is that power should always be distrusted, in whatever hands it is placed.

LETTERS

William Blake (1757-1827)

He who loves his enemies betrays his friends; this surely is
not what Jesus meant.

THE EVERLASTING GOSPEL

Ralph Waldo Emerson (1803-1882)

For every thing you have missed, you have gained something
else; and for every thing you gain, you lose something else.

Alexis de Tocqueville (1805-1859)

America is a land of wonders, in which everything is in
constant motion and every change seems an improvement....
No natural boundary seems to be set to the efforts of man;
and in his eyes, what is not yet done is only what he has not
yet attempted to do.

DEMOCRACY IN AMERICA

Henry Wadsworth Longfellow (1807-1882)

If we could read the secret history of our enemies, we should find in each man's life sorrow and suffering enough to disarm all hostility.

DRIFTWOOD

Shivapuri Baba (1826-1963)

All the things in this universe, men, and materials, all nature and its different phenomena, are simply bewildering. We cannot make out what they are. The reality behind them, the secret of secrets is quite hidden to our view and, as it were, hermetically sealed.

QUOTED IN *LONG PILGRIMAGE*, J. G. BENNETT

Shri Ramakrishna (1836-1886)

This very world is a mansion of mirth; here I can eat, here drink and make merry.

MEDITATIONS

A. E. Housman (1859-1936)

I, a stranger and afraid
In a world I never made.

LAST POEMS

Marie Curie (1867-1934)

You cannot hope to build a better world without improving the individuals. To that end each of us must work for his own improvement, and at the same time share a general responsibility for all humanity, our particular duty being to aid those to whom we think we can be most useful.

PIERRE CURIE

Bertrand Russell (1872-1970)

The secret of happiness is to face the fact that the world is horrible, horrible, "horrible."

QUOTED IN BERTRAND RUSSELL: THE PASSIONATE SCEPTIC, ALAN WOOD

Yogaswami (1872-1964)

If you catch hold of the cat by its tail, it will bite you.
The world will do the same. Live in the world like water
on a lotus leaf.

POSITIVE THOUGHTS FOR DAILY MEDITATION

D. H. Lawrence (1885-1930)

Debacles [such as war or violent revolution] don't save men.
In nearly every case, during the horrors of a catastrophe the
light of integrity and human pride is extinguished in the soul
of the man or the woman involved, and there is left a painful,
unmanned creature, a thing of shame, incapable any more. It
is the great danger of debacles, especially in times of unbelief
like these. Men lack the faith and courage to keep their
souls alert, kindled and unbroken. Afterward there is a great
smouldering of shamed life.

PHOENIX II

T. S. Eliot (1888-1965)

I must tell you that I should really like to think there's
    something wrong with me
Because, if there isn't, then there's something wrong with
    the world itself—and that's much more frightening!

LETTERS

Mikhail Naimy (1889-1988)

Yours is a world divided 'gainst itself, because the "I" in you
is so divided. Yours is a world of barriers and fences, because
the "I" in your is one of barriers and fences. Some things
it would fence out as alien to itself. Some things it would
fence in as kindred to itself. Yet that outside the fence is ever
breaking in; and that within the fence is ever breaking out.

THE BOOK OF MIRDAD

Richard Buckminster Fuller (1895-1983)

I am a passenger on the spaceship, Earth.

OPENING MANUEL FOR SPACESHIP EARTH

J. Krishnamurti (1895–1986)

If you find the garden that you have so carefully cultivated has produced only poisonous weeds, you have to tear them out by the roots; you have to pull down the walls that have sheltered them. You may or may not do it, for you have extensive gardens, cunningly walled-in and well-guarded… but it must be done, for to die rich is to have lived in vain.

NOTEBOOKS

Phyllis McGinley (1905–1978)

We live in the century of the Appeal…. One applauds the industry of professional philanthropy. But it has its dangers. After a while the private heart begins to harden. We fling letters into the wastebasket, are abrupt to telephone solicitations. Charity withers in the incessant gale.

ASPECTS OF SANCTITY

Alan Watts (1915-1973)

Money is a way of measuring wealth but is not wealth in itself. A chest of gold coins or a fat wallet of bills is of no use whatsoever to a wrecked sailor alone on a raft.

THE BOOK–ON THE TABOO AGAINST KNOWING WHO YOU ARE

We do not "come into" this world; we come *out* of it, as leaves from a tree. As the ocean "waves," the universe "peoples." Every individual is an expression of the whole realm of nature, a unique action of the total universe. This fact is rarely, if ever, experienced by most individuals. Even those who know it to be true in theory do not sense or feel it, but continue to be aware of themselves as isolated "egos" inside bags of skin.

THE BOOK–ON THE TABOO AGAINST KNOWING WHO YOU ARE

John F. Kennedy (1917-1963)

The supreme reality of our time is…the vulnerability of our planet.

SPEECH, JUNE 28, 1963

John Collier (1928-1971)

They had what the world has lost: the ancient, lost reverence and passion for human personality joined with the ancient, lost reverence and passion for the earth and its web of life. Since before the Stone Age they have tended that passion as a central, sacred fire. It should be our long hope to renew it in us all.

SPEECH

Osho (1931-1990)

All the religions of the world teach charity, service, giving. But look at the world they have created—there is neither any charity nor any service nor any giving. They have used beautiful words, but their beautiful words are like the words of a blind man who is talking about light.

DISCOURSES

Merit should be decisive, not the power of votes. And the meritorious should be invited because the meritorious are not the ones who are going to beg for votes. A man of merit has a certain dignity. Politicians don't have any dignity. They are beggars.

DISCOURSES

Stopping the world is the whole art of meditation. And to live in the moment is to live in eternity. To taste the moment with no idea, with no mind, is to taste immortality.

THE ORANGE BOOK

Stockholm Conference (1972)

We have forgotten how to be good guests, how to walk lightly on the earth as its other creatures do.

ONLY ONE EARTH

Carlos Castaneda (1925-1998)

This is a weird world.... The forces that guide men are unpredictable, awesome, yet their splendour is something to witness.

JOURNEY TO IXTLAN

Lawrence Durrell (1912-1990)

We are the children of our landscape.

JUSTINE

Marilyn Ferguson (1938-2008)

We have had a profound paradigm shift about the Whole Earth. We know it now as a jewel in space, a fragile water planet. And we have seen that it has no natural borders. It is not the globe of our school days with its many colored nations.

THE AQUARIAN CONSPIRACY

Thomas Moore (Contemporary)

I think we would be able to live in this world more peaceably if our spirituality were to come from looking not just into infinity but very closely at the world around us—and appreciating its depth and divinity.

QUOTED IN *EMBRACING THE EVERYDAY,*
HANDBOOK FOR THE SOUL, EDS. RICHARD CARLSON
AND BENJAMIN SHIELD

Chet Raymo (Contemporary)

The silence of the stars is the silence of creation and re-creation.

THE SOUL OF THE NIGHT

Paolo Soleri (Contemporary)

It is only logical that the pauperization of our soul and the soul of society coincide with the pauperization of the environment. One is the cause and the reflection of the other.

Roger Zelazny (1937–1995)

The universe did not invent justice. Man did. Unfortunately, man must reside in the universe.

THE DREAM MASTER

INDEX